# Financial Forecasting and Modeling

Steven M. Bragg

**Accounting**Tools®

ISBN 9781-64221-216-7

For more information about AccountingTools® products, visit our Web site at www.accountingtools.com.

# Table of Contents

**Chapter 1 - Financial Forecasting**................................................................1

*Uses for Forecasting* ................................................................2

*Forecast Characteristics* ................................................................2

*Implicit and Explicit Forecasts*................................................................3

*Types of Forecasting Methods*................................................................3

*Forecasting Method Selection Criteria* ................................................................6

*Moving Averages*................................................................7

*Exponential Smoothing*................................................................8

*Regression Analysis*................................................................10

*Capture Ratios*................................................................12

*Simple Forecasting Methods* ................................................................13
   Prior Year Actuals × Adjustment Factor ................................................14
   Average of Multiple Prior Periods................................................................15
   Expected Unit Sales Basis ................................................................15
   Spending per Customer ................................................................18
   Change in Advance Bookings or Orders ................................................19

*The Rolling Forecast*................................................................20

*Use of Leading and Lagging Indicators* ................................................................21

*Forecasting Accuracy*................................................................22
   Uncertainty ................................................................22
   Historical Basis................................................................22
   Update Frequency................................................................24
   Biases ................................................................24
   Use of Teams................................................................24
   Nature of Forecasting Model ................................................................25

*Planning Deviations* ................................................................25

*Forecasting Traps* ................................................................25

*Setting Forecast Boundaries* ................................................................26

*Detecting Cresting Sales* ................................................................27

*Evaluation of Forecasts*................................................................29

*Responsibility for Forecasting*................................................................31

**Chapter 2 - Financial Modeling** ................................................................33

*The Financial Statements* ................................................................33
   The Balance Sheet ................................................................33
   The Income Statement................................................................36

The Statement of Cash Flows ...................................................................38

*Interactions between the Financial Statements* .................................*41*

*The Nature of Financial Modeling* .......................................................*42*

*The Financial Modeling Process* ...........................................................*43*

*Key Inputs to the Financial Model* .......................................................*45*

*Structure of the Financial Model* ..........................................................*46*
    Variables Section ........................................................................46

*Fixed Asset and Depreciation Modeling* ..............................................*51*

*Other Assets Modeling* ...........................................................................*53*

*Debt Payable Modeling* ...........................................................................*53*

*Equity Modeling* .......................................................................................*54*

*Balancing the Model* ...............................................................................*54*

*Covenant Monitoring* ...............................................................................*55*

*Working Capital Projections for a Growing Business* ........................*56*

*Working Capital for a Declining Business* ...........................................*58*

*Sensitivity and Scenario Analysis* ........................................................*59*
    Variables Sensitivity ..................................................................59
    Scenario Analysis .......................................................................60
    Excel Tools ..................................................................................61

*Incremental Modeling Analysis* .............................................................*61*

*Model Risk* .................................................................................................*63*
    Budgeting and Planning Software ...........................................65

*Pro Forma Financial Statements* ..........................................................*66*

*Responsibility for Modeling* ...................................................................*66*

**Chapter 3 - Cash Forecasting** ...............................................................**68**

*The Cash Forecast* ...................................................................................*68*
    The Short-Term Cash Forecast .................................................69
    The Medium-Term Cash Forecast ............................................73
    The Long-Term Cash Forecast ..................................................74
    The Use of Averages ..................................................................75

*Automated Cash Forecasting* .................................................................*76*

*The Reliability of Cash Flow Information* .............................................*77*

*The Impact of Special Events* .................................................................*78*

*The Foreign Currency Cash Forecast* ...................................................*79*

*Cash Forecast Reconciliation* .................................................................*79*

**Chapter 4 - Microsoft Excel Modeling**................................................................................**81**

*Moving Averages Function*.............................................................................................*81*

*Exponential Smoothing Function* ...................................................................................*83*

*Linear Trend Function* ...................................................................................................*84*

*Polynomial Trend Function*............................................................................................*86*

*Regression Analysis*.......................................................................................................*87*

*Iterative Calculations Function*.....................................................................................*90*

*Data Table*......................................................................................................................*91*

*Goal Seek*........................................................................................................................*94*

*Scenario Manager* ..........................................................................................................*95*

**Glossary**...................................................................................................................**101**

**Index** .......................................................................................................................**103**

# About the Author

**Steven Bragg, CPA,** has been the chief financial officer or controller of four companies, as well as a consulting manager at Ernst & Young. He received a master's degree in finance from Bentley College, an MBA from Babson College, and a Bachelor's degree in Economics from the University of Maine. He has been a two-time president of the Colorado Mountain Club, and is an avid alpine skier, mountain biker, and certified master diver. Mr. Bragg resides in Centennial, Colorado. He has written more than 300 books and courses, including *New Controller Guidebook*, *GAAP Guidebook*, and *Payroll Management*. He has also written the science fiction novel *Under an Autumn Sun*, first book in *The Auditors* trilogy.

Steven maintains the accountingtools.com web site, which contains continuing professional education courses, the Accounting Best Practices podcast, and thousands of articles on accounting subjects.

# Chapter 1
# Financial Forecasting

## Introduction

Forecasting is the prediction of future events. In the finance field, this usually means that an organization is attempting to predict its future sales. Some amount of forecasting is needed, so that an entity can adequately prepare for future events. For example, if sales are expected to increase significantly, this may call for investments in additional facilities and personnel. Conversely, a projected decline in sales may require advance planning to liquidate assets and sub-lease facilities. If forecasting can provide management with sufficient warning of these future events and with a reasonable degree of accuracy, it is more likely that the most efficient and effective means will be found to prepare for changes. Thus, forecasting can be a key driver of the ability of a firm to generate profits over the long term.

There are several other areas in which financial forecasting can be used, in addition to the prediction of sales. Consider the following opportunities:

- The prediction of corporate results, cash flows, and financial position if different operational and financing decisions are made, such as:
    - Altering the number of days in an organization's receivable credit terms
    - Altering the amount of finished goods kept on hand for use in fulfilling customer orders
    - Altering the number of days in an organization's payable credit terms

- The prediction of corporate cash flows. Cash flow predictions must be as precise as possible, since the treasury staff relies on forecasted cash balances to make investment and borrowing decisions. This high level of precision calls for a unique forecasting system.

We make note of these additional forecasting situations later in the book. The following Financial Modeling chapter covers the construction of a financial model that mimics the financial statements of a business, while the Cash Forecasting chapter addresses the details of how to construct a cash forecast.

## Uses for Forecasting

In what ways can an organization make use of a forecast? As the following bullet points will reveal, the need for a forecast permeates all parts of a company. Forecasting can be used in the following areas:

- *Sales department*. A forecast is needed to determine how many sales regions are required, as well as the number of internal and external salespeople needed to staff the sales regions.
- *Marketing department*. A forecast is used as the basis for scheduling product promotions and other advertising, as well as determining the sales regions within which these activities will take place.
- *Materials management department*. A forecast is used to derive a materials ordering plan, so that contracts can be entered into that ensure adequate supplies. A forecast is also needed to develop a distribution system that includes the sizing, location, configuration, and stocking of regional distribution warehouses.
- *Production department*. A forecast is needed to develop a production plan that will manufacture a sufficient amount of product, in the correct unit totals and product configurations.
- *Human resources department*. A forecast is needed to plan for adequate staffing in all of the other departments, so that a sufficient number of employees are available to achieve all goals.
- *Treasury department*. A sales forecast is a key input into a cash forecast, which is needed to estimate cash inflows and outflows, and the need for and timing of additional financing.

Forecasting is also needed by governments, though for issues other than sales. For example, a city government may need to develop a population forecast, which it can use as the basis for planning roads and utilities.

## Forecast Characteristics

A forecast does not result in a perfect picture of the future. Instead, it only represents a best guess as to what the future may hold for an organization. Given the inherent vagueness of a forecast, it is bound to have the following three characteristics:

- *Accuracy declines over time*. The accuracy of a forecast always declines over time, perhaps to the point where forecasted results are essentially useless. For example, a manufacturer of trendy women's clothes may find that its forecast only generates valid results for the next two months, after which trends may shift and alter actual results to an inordinate degree. Consequently, each entity must find the time period within which its forecasts provide useful information, and not bother with forecasting for longer periods.
- *Aggregation is more accurate*. If an organization tries to forecast at the level of each individual product, it will find that its forecasts cannot consistently

foresee actual results, since customer demand cannot be reliably forecasted at this level of detail. However, if a higher level of aggregation is used, it may be possible to forecast with a fair degree of precision for (for example) an entire product line. One must experiment with different levels of forecasting aggregation to determine which level provides the best mix of usable detail and overall accuracy.

- *Variability from actual results*. Actual results can be expected to vary from the forecast, no matter how expensive or rigorous the forecasting methodology may be. This means that management must plan for a certain amount of variation from the forecast.

It is useful to keep these characteristics in mind when setting expectations for how well a forecasting model will work.

## Implicit and Explicit Forecasts

An explicit forecast is a formal attempt to predict future events. It is typically derived based on the same information sources over time, and is expressed in a standard format. This approach is preferred, since it generates a consistent forecast. An explicit forecast does not necessarily yield results that prove to be accurate, but at least the underlying calculations can be reviewed and adjusted over time.

An implicit forecast is an impromptu forecast that is derived on the spot in order to make a decision. For example, a piece of equipment has failed, and a manager must decide whether to replace it with a similar fixed asset, or one with higher or lower production capacity. If the decision is made to acquire a replacement with a different capacity level, then the manager has made an implicit forecast that the need for the equipment will change in the future. When implicit forecasts are used, they do not usually result in the best decisions, since these forecasts are not based on a systemic approach; instead, they are derived from the guesstimates of the manager involved in making the decision.

## Types of Forecasting Methods

There are a number of forecasting methods that can be used to develop a financial forecast. These methods fall into two general categories, which are quantitative and qualitative. A quantitative approach relies upon quantifiable data, which can then be statistically manipulated. A qualitative approach relies upon information that cannot actually be measured. Examples of quantitative methods are:

- *Causal methods*. These methods assume that the item being forecasted has a cause-and-effect relationship with one or more other variables. For example, the existence of a movie theater can drive sales at a nearby restaurant, so the presence of a blockbuster movie can be expected to increase meal sales in the restaurant. The primary causal analysis method is regression analysis.
- *Time series methods*. These methods derive forecasts based on historical patterns in the data that are observed over equally spaced time intervals. The

assumption is that there is a recurring pattern in the data that will repeat in the future. Three examples of time series methods are:

- o *Rule of thumb.* This is based on a simplified analysis rule, such as copying forward the historical data without alteration. For example, sales for the current month are expected to be the same as the sales generated in the immediately preceding month.
- o *Smoothing.* This approach uses averages of past results, possibly including weightings for more recent data, thereby smoothing out irregularities in the historical data.
- o *Decomposition.* This analysis breaks down the historical data into its trend, seasonal, and cyclical components, and forecasts each one.

## EXAMPLE

Celsius Corporate has recently introduced a new line of remote temperature sensors that use the principles of quantum entanglement to monitor temperature levels thousands of miles away. The company is selling these units at an increasing rate. The sales manager is using a moving average of the last three months of sales to estimate the minimum likely sales level for the next month. Her calculation appears in the following table.

| Month | Actual Sales | 3-Month Moving Average |
|---|---|---|
| January | $300,000 | -- |
| February | 320,000 | -- |
| March | 340,000 | $320,000 |
| April | 342,000 | 334,000 |
| May | 350,000 | 344,000 |
| June | 354,000 | 349,000 |
| July | 360,000 | 355,000 |

Since sales are continuing to increase, the moving average is more useful as an indicator of minimum sales levels than of the actual amount of sales that will be encountered.

**EXAMPLE**

Gatekeeper Corporation runs a toll road. The amount of traffic on the toll road is fairly consistent, though there are random effects that cause toll revenues to bounce around in an irregular manner. The chief financial officer decides to average the results for the immediately preceding six months to forecast an approximate toll revenue figure for the following month. The longer six-month smoothing period is used to minimize the effects of random variations. The analysis appears in the following table.

| Month | Actual Sales | 6-Month Moving Average |
|-------|--------------|------------------------|
| January | $174,000 | -- |
| February | 168,000 | -- |
| March | 175,000 | -- |
| April | 163,000 | -- |
| May | 171,000 | -- |
| June | 167,000 | $170,000 |
| July | 176,000 | 170,000 |

**EXAMPLE**

Nautilus Tours owns several submarines, which it uses to conduct shallow-water tours of coral reefs near major tourist locations. Nautilus has an on-line reservation system that tracks the number of prepaid reserved seats, which are derived from both on-line and telephone sales. This system is the primary source of forecasting information, since it represents "hard" sales for the forecasting period. In addition, the company adds an estimate of additional sales for walk-ins, which is based on a moving average of the number of actual walk-ins that the company has experienced for the past few weeks.

Examples of qualitative methods are:

- *Market research*. This is based on discussions with current and potential customers regarding their need for goods and services. Information must be gathered and analyzed in a systematic manner in order to minimize biases caused by small data sets, inconsistent customer questioning, excessive summarization of data, and so forth. This is an expensive and time-consuming research method. It can be useful for detecting changes in consumer sentiment, which will later be reflected in their buying habits.
- *Opinions of knowledgeable personnel*. This is based on the opinions of those having the greatest and most in-depth knowledge of the information being forecasted. For example, the senior management team may derive forecasts based on their knowledge of the industry. Or, the sales staff may prepare sales forecasts that are based on their knowledge of specific customers. An advantage of using the sales staff for forecasting is that they can provide detailed

forecasts, possibly at the level of the individual customer. There is a tendency for the sales staff to create overly optimistic forecasts.

- *Delphi method.* This is a structured methodology for deriving a forecast from a group of experts, using a facilitator and multiple iterations of analysis to arrive at a consensus opinion. The results from each successive questionnaire are used as the basis for the next questionnaire in each iteration; doing so spreads information among the group if certain information was initially not available to everyone. Given the significant time and effort required, this method is best used for the derivation of longer-term forecasts.

Qualitative methods are especially necessary during the early stages of a company or product, where there is little historical information that can be used as the basis for a quantitative analysis.

## Forecasting Method Selection Criteria

There are a number of criteria to consider when deciding which financial forecasting method to use, including the following:

- *Need for accuracy.* How is the information from a forecast model to be used? If there is no specific need for a highly refined forecast, it makes little sense to bother with the more complex modeling efforts needed to derive this information. For example, if a business merely issues a monthly update to a quarterly rolling forecast that only contains an aggregate sales figure, it can possibly make do with the opinions of its sales department personnel in creating a forecast. Conversely, if there is an intent to probe deep into the data in order to produce many variations on a product, it could make sense to develop individual forecasts for each inventory item.
- *Effort required.* A more rigorous model will probably yield somewhat more accurate forecasts, but at the cost of requiring more forecasting effort. If the difference in outcomes between an advanced method and a simple rule of thumb forecasting method is relatively minor, it can make sense to use the simpler approach.
- *Skill required.* Some forecasting methods can require the use of skilled statisticians or marketing researchers. A smaller organization may not be able to afford the overhead cost associated with these positions.
- *Forecast period.* Is a forecast needed for just a short distance into the future, or is a longer-term forecast needed? In the first case, the emphasis will likely be on a reduced level of effort, since a short-term forecast (such as on a weekly basis) must be revised continually, which will cumulatively require a significant amount of effort. Conversely, a longer-term forecast is only repeated rarely, and so may be worthy of a more detailed forecasting effort.

Quantitative methods might initially appear to be the best approach to forecasting, since they are based on "hard" data. However, there are several situations in which the forecasting outcomes from using these methods are not useful at all. Consider the following situations:

- *No data.* A business may be in startup mode or has just launched an entirely new product line. In either case, there is no initial data set from which a forecast can be generated. In these situations, it can make sense to draw data from similar businesses or products and adapt it for internal use in generating forecasts.
- *Trend continuance assumption.* A core concept driving quantitative methods is that past activity levels will continue into the future. This is by no means always the case. For example, a product line may be reaching a plateau in its sales, followed by a decline in customer orders. In this case, a quantitative analysis based on past data might incorrectly predict a continuing upward trend in sales. A trend may also be impacted by one-time events, such as the flooding of a supplier facility that curtails raw materials and therefore the ability to sell goods.

## Moving Averages

In the earlier Types of Forecasting Methods section, we provided several examples of how moving averages can be used to create a forecast. When should moving averages be used? Their best application is when the historical data does not indicate any cyclical or seasonal component to sales. In addition, there should not be an expectation that the forecast will change significantly. When these conditions are present, a moving average is useful for averaging out the irregular components of historical data over a number of periods. The result is a fairly stable forecast. The Excel tool for calculating a moving average is described in the Moving Averages Function section of the Microsoft Excel Modeling chapter.

**Tip:** Systematically alter the number of periods from which moving average data is taken, and compare the outcome to actual results to determine the optimum number of periods to use for the calculation.

A variation on the concept is the weighted moving average. In this case, the most recent data is considered to be more valuable than older data, so a weighting is assigned to the newer data. An example appears in the following exhibit, where much heavier weightings are given to the immediately preceding two time periods. In the example, a simple average of the three historical periods would have yielded a forecast of $1,000,000. Instead, given the stronger weighting of the final period, the forecast is reduced to $985,000.

**Weighted Moving Average Calculation**

| (000s) | Historical Period 1 | Historical Period 2 | Historical Period 3 | Forecast Period 1 |
|---|---|---|---|---|
| Sales | $1,000 | $1,050 | $950 | --- |
| Weighting points | 10 | 30 | 60 | --- |
| Weighted result | $100 | $315 | $570 | $985 |

The problem with a weighted moving average is that the weighting is entirely subjective. By comparing the results of a weighted moving average forecast to actual results, one can adjust the weighting to improve the accuracy of the forecast.

An implicit weighted moving average occurs when the number of periods over which an average is calculated is shortened. When this happens, the entire weighting is focused on only the few most recent periods, rather than being spread out over a number of periods. The concept is best explained with the following example. A company is forecasting unit sales using a moving average for the past six weeks. Its calculation for the past six weeks is:

$$\frac{500 + 480 + 540 + 535 + 570 + 585}{6} = 535$$

In this calculation, the weighting is spread evenly over each of the past six weeks. The formula is then changed, so that it only encompasses the past three weeks of unit sales. The formula now changes to:

$$\frac{535 + 570 + 585}{3} = 563$$

In effect, the final three weeks have cumulatively been awarded a 100% weighting, while the preceding three weeks were given a 0% weighting. Consequently, altering the number of periods used in a moving average calculation effectively results in a weighting of the model.

A problem with any type of moving average forecasting system is that detailed records must be kept of the relevant financial information from which forecasts are being calculated.

## Exponential Smoothing

Exponential smoothing is a forecasting method that is based on historical patterns in the data. It is a time series method, as defined earlier in the Types of Forecasting Methods section. This method employs a *smoothing constant* in combination with recent and actual forecasted activity to derive a forecast. A smoothing constant determines the level at which actual experience influences a forecast. Thus, if a prior forecast was too high, the smoothing constant is used to reduce the forecast in the next period. Conversely, if a prior forecast was too low, the smoothing constant increases the forecast in the next period. The smoothing constant should be low if the pattern of sales has been relatively stable in the past. The smoothing constant increases in size if there have been large changes in sales. The smoothing constant is inserted into the following formula to derive a forecast:

$$\begin{array}{c}\text{New}\\\text{Forecast}\end{array} = \begin{array}{c}\text{Past}\\\text{Forecast}\end{array} + \begin{array}{c}\text{Smoothing}\\\text{Constant}\end{array} \times \left( \begin{array}{c}\text{Actual}\\\text{Demand}\end{array} - \begin{array}{c}\text{Past}\\\text{Forecast}\end{array} \right)$$

The information requirements for exponential smoothing are quite limited. It is only necessary to employ the data from the prior two periods in order to derive the smoothing constant. The calculation of the smoothing constant is as follows:

$$\frac{\text{Period 2 forecast} - \text{Period 1 forecast}}{\text{Period 1 actual demand} - \text{Period 1 forecast}}$$

---

**EXAMPLE**

Grizzly Golf Carts uses exponential smoothing in its financial forecasting. In January, Grizzly forecasted that customers would order 300 of its golf carts. Actual demand was 330 carts. The February forecast is that 315 carts will be ordered. The company's forecaster uses this information to derive the smoothing constant, which is calculated as follows:

$$\frac{315 \text{ Carts forecasted in February} - 300 \text{ Carts forecasted in January}}{330 \text{ Carts ordered in January} - 300 \text{ Carts forecasted in January}}$$

$$= 0.5 \text{ Smoothing constant}$$

**EXAMPLE**

Green Lawn Care forecasted customer orders of 500 electric lawn mowers in the past week, and actual demand for that week was 490 mowers. The company's smoothing constant is 0.2. The company uses the following exponential smoothing calculation to derive the following forecast for the next week:

$$\begin{array}{c}\text{New}\\\text{Forecast}\end{array} = \begin{array}{c}500 \text{ Units}\\\text{Past}\\\text{Forecast}\end{array} + \begin{array}{c}0.2\\\text{Smoothing}\\\text{Constant}\end{array} \times \left( \begin{array}{c}490 \text{ Units}\\\text{Actual}\\\text{Demand}\end{array} - \begin{array}{c}500 \text{ Units}\\\text{Past}\\\text{Forecast}\end{array} \right)$$

$$= 498 \text{ Mowers}$$

In essence, the company is using a modest smoothing constant to slightly reduce its forecast for the next period, since the actual demand in the past week was lower than expected.

---

Excel provides a tool to generate exponential smoothing forecasts, which is explained in the Microsoft Excel Modeling chapter.

## Regression Analysis

Regression analysis is a forecasting method that is based on a cause-and-effect relationship between a dependent and independent variable. The two factors involved in this analysis are:

- *Independent variable*. This is a variable that is not impacted by any other variables being measured.
- *Dependent variable*. This variable is impacted by other variables. An independent variable can cause changes in a dependent variable, but a dependent variable cannot cause changes in an independent variable.

As examples of independent and dependent variables, a person's income (the independent variable) impacts the amount of the individual's spending (the dependent variable). Or, the price of a product (the independent variable) impacts the number of units sold (the dependent variable).

This type of analysis only yields accurate results when the variables used are reliable indicators of an activity. The level of this reliability can be measured using the *correlation coefficient*, for which the formula is:

$$r = \frac{n(\sum xy) - (\sum x)(\sum y)}{\sqrt{[n(\sum x^2) - (\sum x)^2][n(\sum y^2) - (\sum y)^2]}}$$

The symbols in the preceding formula are explained as follows:

x = Independent variable
y = Dependent variable
n = Number of observations

The result of the formula ("r") is a value between negative one and positive one, where a value closer to positive one represents a tight relationship between the dependent and independent variables. The following table illustrates how the output of the correlation coefficient calculation can be interpreted.

**Strength of Correlation Coefficient**

| R Value | Level of Relationship |
|---|---|
| Positive 0.70 or higher | Very strong positive relationship |
| Positive 0.40 – 0.69 | Strong positive relationship |
| Positive 0.30 – 0.39 | Moderate positive relationship |
| Positive 0.20 – 0.29 | Weak positive relationship |
| Positive 0.01 – 0.19 | Minimal positive relationship |
| Zero | No relationship |
| Negative 0.01 – 0.19 | Minimal negative relationship |
| Negative 0.20 – 0.29 | Weak negative relationship |
| Negative 0.30 – 0.39 | Moderate negative relationship |
| Negative 0.40 – 0.69 | Strong negative relationship |
| Negative 0.70 or lower | Very strong negative relationship |

Once an independent variable has been found that closely correlates with the dependent variable, a line can be plotted through the data using the following formula for a straight line:

$$Y = a + bx$$

The symbols in the preceding formula are explained as follows:

> Y = Dependent variable
> a = Intercept point of the regression line and the y axis
> b = Slope of the regression line
> x = Independent variable

---

### EXAMPLE

The Sojourn Hotel and Spa has established a strong positive relationship between the number of room guests and the number of spa treatments in the adjacent spa. An analysis of the data results in the following equation that graphs the regression analysis:

$$Y = 100 + 1.55(x)$$

For example, if there are 1,000 room guests in a given period, then the number of spa treatments is estimated to be as follows:

$$Y = 100 + 1.55(1,000)$$

$$= 1,650 \text{ Spa treatments}$$

The calculation indicates that 100 spa treatments are conducted that are not related to room guests, and that each guest pays for an average of 1.55 spa treatments.

---

An examination of a regression calculation may find that the earlier or later data points used to plot a line result in a closer fit with the line. If so, it can make sense to assign a weighting to the data points, so that those points assigned a higher weighting are factored more heavily into the regression calculation, and those weighted less have a lesser impact on the outcome. For example, a weighting of 1.0 has no impact, while a weighting of 0.7 reduces the impact of a data point, and a weighting of 1.3 increases the impact. The most common application of this concept is to assign a reduced weighting to the oldest data points, so that more recent data is given more weight in the calculation of a fitted line.

The concept of plotting a best-fit line is dealt with in more detail in the Linear Trend Function and Polynomial Trend Function sections in the Microsoft Excel Modeling chapter.

A more advanced form of regression analysis is multiple regression analysis, where the impact of two or more independent variables on a dependent variable is analyzed. For example, forecasts could be derived for:

- Sales of Hawaiian helicopter tours that are based on the impact of an advertising campaign *and* the number of visitors to the islands.
- Sales of consumer goods that are based on the impact of advertising frequency *and* the type of media used.
- Sales of freemium products that are based on the price at which the premium product is offered *and* the features offered in the free product.

A multiple regression analysis should be used when a simple regression does not result in a sufficiently high R value to show a strong relationship between a single independent variable and the dependent variable.

The Regression tool in Excel can be used to obtain information about the relevance of the data used for a multiple regression analysis. See the Regression Analysis section in the Microsoft Excel modeling chapter for more information.

## Capture Ratios

A key part of many financial forecasts is the *capture ratio*. This is the proportion of customers initially attracted to a company's products that eventually make a purchase. The ratio can be devised in different ways, depending on the industry. For example:

- The number of customers visiting a dealer showroom that eventually buy a car
- The number of hotel room guests who buy a meal at the adjacent restaurant
- The number of visitors to a company's website that make a purchase

When there is a strong capture ratio associated with a company's sales efforts, it is essential to incorporate it into short-term forecasts, since it can explain the bulk of these sales.

---

**EXAMPLE**

Glow Atomic has found that 8% of the visitors to its web site store will purchase the company's baseball-sized portable fusion generators. In addition, twenty purchases per month are made via walk-in sales at the company's headquarters store. In the upcoming month, Glow expects 10,000 visitors to its web site. This traffic results in the following forecast calculation for units sold:

Total units forecast = 20 Walk-in sales + 0.08 Capture ratio (10,000 Web site visitors)

= 820 Units forecast

---

## Simple Forecasting Methods

We have already described several relatively advanced forecasting methods. Given the level of complexity involved, many organizations do not use them. Instead, they employ a variety of simplified techniques that require little analysis work and minimal forecasting knowledge. Examples of these methods are noted in the following exhibit.

### Simple Forecasting Methods

| Method | Commentary |
|---|---|
| Prior year actuals × Adjustment factor | Likely the most common forecasting method, where the prior period actual results are expected to repeat in the current period, possibly adjusted for any number of factors such as expectations of an industry downturn or the introduction of a new product line. |
| Prior year budget × Adjustment factor | Only yields useful results if the prior year budget closely predicted actual results. This is most likely to be the case in a low-growth industry where long-term results are highly predictable. |
| Average of multiple prior periods | Works well when there is no significant trend in sales, but rather a sales level that moves up and down moderate amounts from period to period. Should not be used when there is a clear upward, downward, or seasonal trend in the historical data. |
| Expected unit sales basis | The sales department creates a detailed unit forecast at the level of the individual product, and calculates sales dollars based on the expected selling price. This approach works well in a stable market where product life cycles are long and there is little pricing pressure. |
| Spending per customer | Works well when each customer buys a consistent average amount per forecasting period. However, it can yield inaccurate results when the business switches to a new market segment in which customer spending habits are different. |
| Change in advance bookings or orders | Useful when advance bookings or orders are considered a strong indicator of future sales. Works well in seasonal businesses such as hotels and resorts, or for consumer products for which there is significant marketing support. |

Some of the methods listed in the preceding table are described further in the following subsections.

13

**Prior Year Actuals × Adjustment Factor**

The use of the prior year's actual results as the basis for a forecast is probably the most common forecasting method, for the following two reasons:

- The forecast is based on an aggregate figure that is derived from all types of sales, which requires little effort to compile (as opposed to the later sub-section describing the expected unit sales basis).
- The entity has already achieved the prior year sales figure, so there is no question that the required market share exists and that the organization has the capacity to meet the indicated sales level.

The management team can then add to or subtract from the prior year actual results for any number of factors that are expected to take place during the forecast period, such as:

- Product price changes
- Additions to production capacity
- Certain customers will be added or dropped
- New sales regions will be added
- New product lines will be added
- New distribution channels will be added

The adjustments to the prior year actuals may be the most difficult to predict, especially if the organization is making changes for which there is no history, such as an entirely new product line.

This forecasting method does not work well when a business' products are subject to short life cycles, and especially when there is little corporate or product branding that will attract and retain customers over the long term. In this situation, sales levels may spike and drop at irregular intervals, with no consistent sales level that can be predicted forward into the next year.

---

**EXAMPLE**

Rubens Trailers specializes in the production of double-wide trailers. Sales of these trailers have proven to be remarkably consistent over the past decade, featuring a modest 2% average growth rate, though demand in the past year came close to maxing out the company's production capacity. For the upcoming year, Rubens has invested in an oversized new production facility that can handle a weighty increase in production.

In the past year, the company had $40 million of sales. The capacity problem will no longer be an issue, so there is an expectation of an additional 2% increase in sales to match the long-term trend, which is $800,000. In addition, the company is launching a standard-width trailer that it hopes will achieve $5 million in sales. Since this is a new product for which there are many competing products, there is considerable uncertainty about the $5 million figure. Thus, Rubens has a $40.8 million component to its forecast that it considers to be solid, and a $5 million component from which actual results may vary a great deal.

---

## Average of Multiple Prior Periods

A business that is locked into a relatively flat revenue pattern can consider using an average of several prior periods as its forecasting method. This method may work well for governments, which typically service relatively flat population levels for long periods of time (in the absence of new residential construction). The same can be said for businesses that have monopolies or near-monopolies, but which are restricted from operating outside of their core areas, such as regulated utilities.

### EXAMPLE

The Waiakea Botanical Gardens are located in Hawaii. The gardens are famous for their outrageously large plant life, which is fed by an ideal mix of morning sun and afternoon rain. The gardens serve a consistent client base of gardening devotees who come from all over the world. There is no upward or downward trend in the number of customers in any given year, so the garden's bookkeeper uses the following simple method to average sales for the past three years in order to forecast the most likely sales level for the coming year:

|  | 2 Years Ago | 1 Year Ago | Current Year | Next Year |
|---|---|---|---|---|
| Sales | $450,000 | $462,000 | $440,000 | $451,000 |

## Expected Unit Sales Basis

A unit-based sales forecast contains an itemization of a company's sales expectations for the forecast period, which may be in both units and dollars. If a company has a large number of products, it usually aggregates its expected sales into a smaller number of product categories; otherwise, the forecasting process becomes too unwieldy.

The basic calculation in the revenue forecast is to itemize the number of unit sales expected in one row of the forecast, and then list the average expected unit price in the next row, with the total revenues appearing in the third row. If any sales discounts or returns are anticipated, these items are also listed in the forecast.

### EXAMPLE

Quest Adventure Gear is a maker of rugged travel gear. One of its equipment lines is a propane-powered camp stove. Its revenue forecast is as follows:

|  | Quarter 1 | Quarter 2 | Quarter 3 | Quarter 4 | Total |
|---|---|---|---|---|---|
| Forecasted unit sales | 5,500 | 6,000 | 7,000 | 8,000 | 26,500 |
| × Price per unit | $35 | $35 | $38 | $38 | -- |
| = Total gross sales | $192,500 | $210,000 | $266,000 | $304,000 | $972,500 |
| - Sales discounts and allowances | -3,850 | -$4,200 | -$5,320 | -6,080 | -19,450 |
| = Total net sales | $188,650 | $205,800 | $260,680 | $297,920 | $953,050 |

Quest's sales manager expects that increased demand in the second half of the year will allow it to increase its wholesale unit price from $35 to $38. Also, the sales manager expects that the company's historical sales discounts and allowances percentage of two percent of gross sales will continue through the forecast period.

---

This revenue forecast example only incorporates a single product, which results in a very simplistic forecast. Realistically, most companies sell many products and services, and must find a way to aggregate them into a forecast that strikes a balance between revealing a reasonable level of detail and not overwhelming the reader with a massive list of line-item projections. There are several ways to aggregate information to meet this goal.

One approach is to summarize revenue information by sales territory, as shown in the following exhibit. This approach is most useful when the primary source of information for the revenue forecast is the sales managers of the various territories, and is particularly important if the company is planning to close down or open up new sales territories; changes at the territory level may be the primary drivers of changes in sales. In the example, the Central Plains sales territory is expected to be launched midway through the forecast year and to contribute modestly to total sales volume by year end.

**Sample Revenue Forecast by Territory**

| Territory | Quarter 1 | Quarter 2 | Quarter 3 | Quarter 4 | Total |
|---|---|---|---|---|---|
| Northeast | $135,000 | $141,000 | $145,000 | $132,000 | $553,000 |
| Mid-Atlantic | 200,000 | 210,000 | 208,000 | 195,000 | 813,000 |
| Southeast | 400,000 | 425,000 | 425,000 | 395,000 | $1,645,000 |
| Central Plains | 0 | 0 | 100,000 | 175,000 | 275,000 |
| Rocky Mountain | 225,000 | 235,000 | 242,000 | 230,000 | 932,000 |
| West Coast | 500,000 | 560,000 | 585,000 | 525,000 | 2,170,000 |
| Totals | $1,460,000 | $1,571,000 | $1,705,000 | $1,652,000 | $6,388,000 |

Another approach is to summarize revenue information by contract, as shown below. This is realistically the only viable way to structure the revenue forecast in situations where a company is heavily dependent upon a set of contracts that have definite ending dates. In this situation, divide the forecast into existing and projected contracts, with subtotals for each type of contract, in order to separately show firm revenues and less-likely revenues. This type of forecast is commonly used when a company is engaged in services or government work.

## Sample Revenue Forecast by Contract

| Contract | Quarter 1 | Quarter 2 | Quarter 3 | Quarter 4 | Total |
|---|---|---|---|---|---|
| **Existing Contracts:** | | | | | |
| Air Force #01327 | $175,000 | $175,000 | $25,000 | $-- | $375,000 |
| Coast Guard #AC124 | 460,000 | 460,000 | 460,000 | 25,000 | 1,405,000 |
| Marines #BG0047 | 260,000 | 280,000 | 280,000 | 260,000 | 1,080,000 |
| Subtotal | $895,000 | $915,000 | $765,000 | $285,000 | $2,860,000 |
| | | | | | |
| **Projected Contracts:** | | | | | |
| Air Force resupply | $-- | $-- | $150,000 | $300,000 | $450,000 |
| Army training | -- | 210,000 | 600,000 | 550,000 | 1,360,000 |
| Marines software | 10,000 | 80,000 | 80,000 | 100,000 | 270,000 |
| Subtotal | $10,000 | $290,000 | $830,000 | $950,000 | $2,080,000 |
| | | | | | |
| Totals | $905,000 | $1,205,000 | $1,595,000 | $1,235,000 | $4,940,000 |

Yet another approach for a company having a large number of products is to aggregate them into product lines, and then create a summary-level forecast at the product line level. This approach is shown below. However, if a revenue forecast is created for product lines, also consider creating a supporting schedule of projected sales for each of the products within that product line, in order to properly account for the timing and revenue volumes associated with the ongoing introduction of new products and cancellation of old ones. An example of such a supporting schedule is also shown below, itemizing the "Alpha" line item in the product line revenue forecast. Note that this schedule provides detail about the launch of a new product (the Alpha Windmill) and the termination of another product (the Alpha Methane Converter) that are crucial to the formulation of the total revenue figure for the product line.

## Sample Revenue Forecast by Product Line

| Product Line | Quarter 1 | Quarter 2 | Quarter 3 | Quarter 4 | Total |
|---|---|---|---|---|---|
| Product line alpha | $450,000 | $500,000 | $625,000 | $525,000 | $2,100,000 |
| Product line beta | 100,000 | 110,000 | 150,000 | 125,000 | 485,000 |
| Product line charlie | 250,000 | 250,000 | 300,000 | 300,000 | 1,100,000 |
| Product line delta | 80,000 | 60,000 | 40,000 | 20,000 | 200,000 |
| Totals | $880,000 | $920,000 | $1,115,000 | $970,000 | $3,885,000 |

**Sample Supporting Schedule for the Revenue Forecast by Product Line**

| | Quarter 1 | Quarter 2 | Quarter 3 | Quarter 4 | Total |
|---|---|---|---|---|---|
| **Alpha product line detail:** | | | | | |
| Alpha Flywheel | $25,000 | $35,000 | $40,000 | $20,000 | $120,000 |
| Alpha Generator | 175,000 | 225,000 | 210,000 | 180,000 | 790,000 |
| Alpha Windmill | -- | -- | 200,000 | 250,000 | 450,000 |
| Alpha Methane Converter | 150,000 | 140,000 | 25,000 | -- | 315,000 |
| Alpha Nuclear Converter | 100,000 | 100,000 | 150,000 | 75,000 | 425,000 |
| Totals | $450,000 | $500,000 | $625,000 | $525,000 | $2,100,000 |

A danger in constructing a supporting schedule for a product line forecast is that one can delve too deeply into all of the various manifestations of a product, resulting in an inordinately large and detailed schedule. This situation might arise when a product comes in many colors or options. In such cases, engage in as much aggregation at the individual product level as necessary to yield a schedule that is not *excessively* detailed. It is nearly impossible to forecast revenue at the level of the color or specific option mix associated with a product, so it makes little sense to create a schedule at that level of detail.

## Spending per Customer

Forecasting based on the average spend per customer works well when customers buy a consistent amount per forecasting period. This approach can yield the most consistent results when essential goods are being sold on a repetitive basis, such as food sales by a grocery store. In this scenario, a business probably services customers within a specifically-defined geographic region, who have limited alternative purchasing options. Another example is an agricultural supply store in a farming district where the nearest competing store is 50 miles away.

For more precision in the forecast, it can make sense to stratify customers, since the top and bottom groups of customers may spend substantially different amounts than the median group.

---

**EXAMPLE**

Lonely Lake Lodge is the only purveyor of foodstuffs within a 20-mile radius in the backwoods of Minnesota. The owner's customers are comprised of two distinct groups, which are the 500 permanent residents of the area, and the 2,000 campers who descend on the area during the summer months. The spending habits of these two groups are entirely different, as outlined by the sales forecast in the following table, which identifies spending by each type of customer for each season of the upcoming year.

| | Winter | Spring | Summer | Fall |
|---|---|---|---|---|
| Full-time residents | 480 | 500 | 500 | 480 |
| × Spending/each | $1,200 | $1,000 | $1,000 | $1,200 |
| Full-timer spending | $576,000 | $500,000 | $500,000 | $576,000 |
| | | | | |
| Seasonal residents | 50 | 750 | 2,000 | 200 |
| × Spending/each | $200 | $150 | $150 | $200 |
| Seasonal spending | $10,000 | $112,500 | $300,000 | $40,000 |
| | | | | |
| Grand total spending | $586,000 | $612,500 | $800,000 | $616,000 |

## Change in Advance Bookings or Orders

Forecasting based on changes in advance bookings or orders is an essential tool in the tourism industry, especially in those areas where travel plans are made months in advance. If advance bookings are down, this likely means that a resort will need to offer cut-rate deals to bring in vacationers at the last minute, which reduces overall revenues. Conversely, an increase in advance bookings may allow a business to increase its last-minute rates for any residual capacity, thereby boosting revenues.

### EXAMPLE

The Saba Dive Resort caters entirely to scuba divers, who enjoy the pristine underwater views off the southwest coast of the island. It is now July, and the Caribbean has already been hit by four hurricanes, with additional storms queued up off the coast of Africa and headed towards the Caribbean – and the Saba Dive Resort.

The resort's bookkeeper is attempting to forecast sales for September, when hurricane season will be at its peak. To do so, she reviews the changes in advance bookings for September, and notes that 20% of these bookings have been cancelled, likely due to the nervousness of divers regarding how the hurricane season is trending.

The resort also earns revenue from day-trippers who fly in from St. Maarten with little advance warning. She assumes that the September numbers for this group will drop by an equivalent amount, for the same reason. Her forecast is based on the resort's actual results for the preceding September, which results in the following forecast detail:

| | September Actual Preceding Year | September Forecast Current Year |
|---|---|---|
| Revenue from advance bookings | $380,000 | $304,000 |
| Revenue from day trippers | 50,000 | 40,000 |
| Total Revenue | $430,000 | $344,000 |

## The Rolling Forecast

A rolling forecast is a recasting of a company's sales on a frequent basis. The frequency of forecasting means that the forecast could potentially occupy a central role in a company's planning activities. In this section we address the timing of updates and the time period covered.

Ideally, a rolling forecast could be created as soon as a company issues its financial statements for the most recent reporting period. By doing so, management can update the existing forecast based in part on the information contained in the most recent financial statements. It may be tempting to update the forecast on a monthly basis, but do so only if the resulting information is useful to management – which is usually only the case in a volatile market. In most situations, a quarterly update to the forecast is sufficient, and is not looked upon as quite so much of a chore by the management team. An alternative view of when to update a forecast is whenever there is a significant triggering event. This may be a change in the business environment, the release of a new product, the loss of a key employee, and so forth. If management is updating only after a triggering event, the revision of a rolling forecast may be quite sporadic.

Another issue with the rolling forecast is the time period to be covered by it. There is no universally correct period. Instead, the time period covered depends on the nature of the business. Here are several examples of situations calling for different forecast periods:

- *Software development.* A business creates software and launches it through the Internet. Its investment in fixed assets is low. In this case, competing products can appear at any time, and the market can pivot in a new direction at a moment's notice. If so, management probably does not need a forecast that extends more than three months into the future.
- *Market leading manufacturer.* A business is the dominant low-cost provider of industrial goods in its market niche, thanks to its heavy investment in fixed assets and production technology. The market is probably steady and changes little, so management can get by with a quarterly forecast update that extends over a two-year period.
- *Government contractor.* A company has a backlog of long-term contracts with the federal government. Its cost structure is easily predicted, and revenues are based largely on contracts that are already in hand. Management probably only needs a quarterly forecast update, with particular emphasis on the revenues generated by specific contracts. The forecast duration should match the duration of key contracts.
- *Retail business.* A company sells fashion-oriented retail goods from multiple stores. Sales levels are highly variable, so management probably needs a monthly forecast that has a particular emphasis on sales by product line and by store.

Another way to view the duration of the forecast period is whether extending it further into the future will alter any management decision making. If not, there is no point in creating the extended forecast. A good way to determine the correct duration is to start with a rolling 12-month forecast and adjust the duration after a few months to more closely fit the needs of management. It is quite common to have a forecast duration of at least one year, and rarely more than two years.

## Use of Leading and Lagging Indicators

A set of information that can influence the outcome of forecasts is leading and lagging indicators. A leading indicator is something that can be used to predict future economic behavior, while a lagging indicator occurs after the economy has begun to follow a trend. Clearly, leading indicators are of the most use for forecasting purposes, though lagging indicators can be used to reinforce other information sources regarding established trends. Many leading and lagging indicators are available for the economy, including the following:

- *Consumer price index.* Indicates changes in the inflation rate, which can impact the cost of materials and the prices charged to customers.
- *Construction spending.* Can be used to predict future gross domestic product numbers, since it is a major component of the economy.
- *Gross domestic product.* Provides a general view of the health of the economy. A downward trend can signal the start of a recession.
- *Housing starts.* Trends in the number of new residential construction projects started are indicators of a strengthening or weakening economy.
- *Interest rates.* Increases in lending rates negatively impact business and consumer spending, while strong rate reductions have the reverse impact.
- *Producer price index.* Changes in the prices charged to manufacturers indicate variations in the rate of inflation or deflation. This index is from the perspective of producers, while the consumer price index is from the perspective of consumers.
- *S&P 500 stock index.* Gives a general indication of the direction of the U.S. economy, for which it is considered a leading indicator.
- *Initial unemployment claims.* An increase in initial claims for unemployment insurance signals the start of a decline in economic conditions. It is considered a leading indicator.
- *Unemployment rate.* Tends to confirm the direction of the economy, as it is considered a lagging indicator.

These items should certainly be plotted on a trend line, so that management can see longer-term trends in the data. Of particular interest is when there are several consecutive months of an upward or downward trend that contravenes the established trend. Multiple months of a change in direction indicates an underlying shift in economic activity. For example, housing starts have been growing for the past four years, but there has now been a declining trend in housing starts for the past three months. This can be considered an indicator of an upcoming recession.

The information presented by leading and lagging indicators is one of many inputs that can be considered when constructing a financial forecast. It is not necessarily the central data item to consider, since the typical organization may depend on other factors to derive its revenues. For example, a government contractor may have several long-term contracts with the military for which it is the only supplier, and so it is not overly concerned with general economic conditions. Nonetheless, leading and lagging indicators can be used to deliberately skew forecasts up or down.

## Forecasting Accuracy

Forecasting deals with the future, and so is inherently inaccurate. In most cases, there will always be some variation between the amount forecasted and actual results, no matter how refined the forecasting methodology may be. This level of inherent inaccuracy changes with the duration of the forecast. For example, a forecast that only extends one day into the future is likely based on existing on-hand orders, and so will be vastly more accurate than the far end of a one-year forecast that is based on general impressions of customer demand. Thus, a forecast for a period well into the future will always yield less reliable information than a shorter-term forecast.

We note several issues impacting forecasting accuracy in the following sub-sections.

### Uncertainty

A major driver of forecasting accuracy is uncertainty. If management were to have perfect knowledge of future conditions, it could generate remarkably accurate forecasts. However, this is rarely the case. Instead, there may be any number of uncertainties, such as the possible bankruptcy of a customer, the impact of a looming recession on customer demand, and the entry of new competitors into the market.

### Historical Basis

The typical starting point for a financial forecast is historical information. That is, the trend of historical information may be extended into the future, adjusted for various factors such as an expected decline in economic activity.

---

**EXAMPLE**

Eskimo Construction builds structures that are designed for cold environments. The company has enjoyed a consistent growth pattern for the past ten years that has resulted in an average of 8% growth per year. The CFO is reviewing initial sales estimates for the next year that incorporate this 8% trend. She decides to reduce the growth rate to zero, based on the effects of climate change that are no longer requiring customers to demand the cold weather building features that Eskimo specializes in.

---

There may be an underlying pattern within historical information that can be incorporated into a forecast. These patterns are as follows:

- *Trend.* This is a long-term projection of increases or decreases in activity levels contained within the historical information. Trends can be inaccurate if the underlying drivers of financial patterns change from their historical levels.
- *Seasonal.* This is a periodic change that follows a consistent pattern. For example, a snow shovel manufacturer experiences a sales spike in the winter, while a patio furniture manufacturer sells the bulk of its goods during the spring and summer months. Seasonality may even apply to individual days of the week; for example, a bar may experience its highest volume on Fridays and Saturdays. Seasonal changes tend to be fairly predictable.
- *Cyclical.* This is long-term movements around the trend line that occur over periods of more than one year. An example of cyclicality is when an industry periodically creates too much production capacity, which leads to sharp price declines and the departures of competitors from the industry. The timing and extent of cyclicality tends to be difficult to predict.

These patterns are shown in the following chart. In addition, historical data contains random fluctuations that are caused by unsystematic short-term events.

**Trend, Seasonal, and Cyclical Patterns**

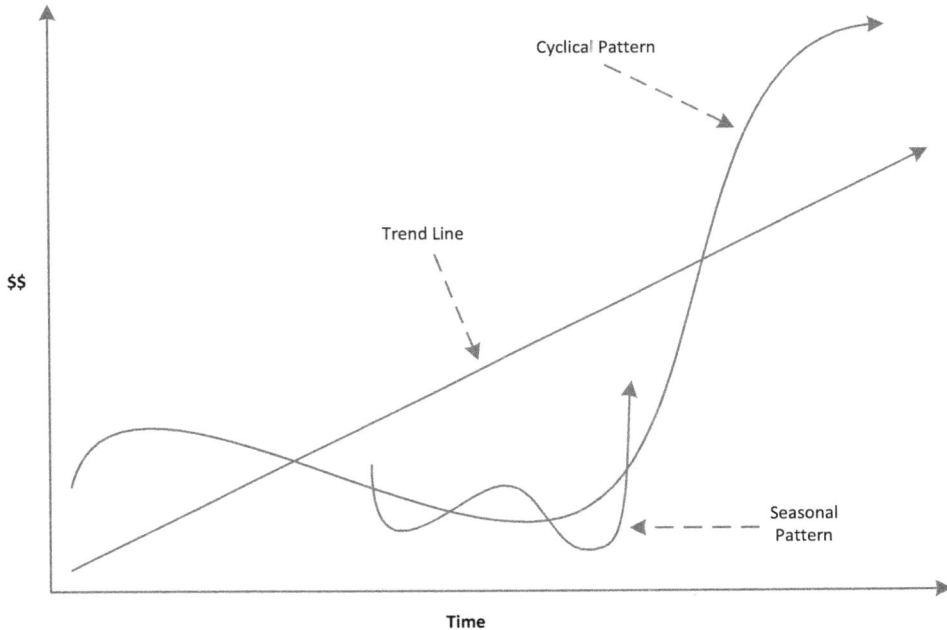

## Update Frequency

Financial forecasts are inherently more accurate if they are updated on a regular basis. The increase in the level of accuracy will depend upon the thoroughness of the update; thus, a cursory examination may not yield much of an accuracy improvement. Update frequency plays a particularly important role in the forecasts used in the annual budget. Since the annual budget is not usually updated during the budget year, the forecasts for the last few months of the budget year are more likely to be quite inaccurate when compared to actual results. This issue can be mitigated by revising the budget at more frequent intervals.

## Biases

The person conducting a forecasting exercise will likely have several biases that skew how she interprets the information. For example, the person may give more credence to information that confirms her beliefs, while discounting information that challenges her conclusions. These biases may impact which information is included in a trend analysis, or how the results are interpreted.

A particular concern is *durability bias*, which is the tendency to project the recent past into the future. The assumption is that recent trends are likely to continue, which is not necessarily the case. Recent occurrences may have been triggered by one-time events that are unlikely to recur, such as a major order from a buyer for a fashion item. Or, the billings under a large government contract have nearly consumed the original funding, after which the contract will be terminated. These issues are routinely overlooked by people, who prefer to extrapolate recent sales figures into the future without looking at the underlying trends.

To avoid durability bias, one must examine every component and assumption relating to a project or business, to see if the extrapolation is reasonable. Organizations that do the best job of avoiding durability bias constantly question their growth rate assumptions. They also pay close attention to leading indicators within their industries, to catch any hint of a change in the future direction. It can also be useful to review the forecasts of anyone with a deep knowledge of the industry for insights into likely changes in future directions.

## Use of Teams

Teams generally come up with better forecasts than individuals, especially when there is a significant diversity in the team membership. In particular, several generalists should be included on the team, since they are more likely to challenge the presumed experts, quite possibly providing insights that an expert would miss. However, this forecasting improvement only works if there is a high degree of trust amongst the team members, so that everyone is encouraged to give their opinions, and those opinions are duly considered.

**Nature of Forecasting Model**

Forecasting accuracy is determined to a considerable extent by the nature of the forecasting model. If a forecast is merely based on a percentage change from historical information, the result will be insufficiently sophisticated to be an indicator of actual future results. If the forecasting model delves into greater detail, then the accuracy level is likely to be higher. For example, a forecaster could incorporate into a model the impact of any bottlenecks within the business, or the effects of a marketing campaign, or the expected termination date of a customer contract.

## Planning Deviations

The management team may find that its forecasts vary from actual results within a certain band of outcomes. For example, the financial forecast may consistently fall within a range of 20% of actual results, both above and below the actual results. If the band within which deviations fall is relatively consistent, it may be useful to prepare budgets based on the high and low band limits, as well as for the forecasted amount. By doing so, management can be prepared for the full range of outcomes that are likely to occur.

## Forecasting Traps

A common trap that companies fall into when forecasting rapid growth is to account for the delaying effect of *pacing*. From the perspective of forecasting, pacing is the rate at which an entity can ramp up an operational issue until it can handle a target revenue level. Here are several pacing scenarios to consider:

- *Sales staff.* A company sells a product that requires an intensive hands-on sale by an experienced salesperson. The company must delay forecasted revenues that are associated with new salespeople until such time as they are capable of selling at the same success rate as more experienced salespeople. This is one of the most significant pacing issues.
- *Selling cycle.* In some industries, customers only buy products at a certain pace. This is particularly true for large capital products, where purchases are only considered once a year, and must go through a lengthy review process before a purchase order is issued. In such situations, a company may hire a group of excellent, well-trained sales people, and yet not earn a single new customer order for a long time.
- *Retail roll out.* A company has developed an excellent retail concept store, and can gain sales rapidly if it can roll out the concept into new locations as fast as possible. This is a major pacing issue, since the company likely has only a small number of people who are sufficiently skilled in store openings, and that group can only open a certain number of stores within a given period of time.
- *Production facilities.* If a company can only gain new sales after it builds new production facilities, it cannot forecast more sales until the facilities are

complete and tested, and the new staff hired for the facility is capable of running it at the planned level of productivity. The variety of issues involved can mean that new sales cannot begin until a long time after a facility has been constructed.

- *Permits*. A company can only do business in a new sales region after it obtains all necessary government permits. This is a particular problem when a business is attempting to gain entry into a new country where it has few contacts or local partners.
- *New technology*. A company has created a product that has cutting-edge technology. Such products tend to have a higher failure rate until the engineering and production staffs can figure out the underlying issues. This process of working out the kinks can greatly delay revenue generation.

Pacing is an important topic that less seasoned managers tend to ignore. The result is a revenue forecast that initially appears reasonable, but which a company is not able to meet, due to a lack of attention to underlying factors that exert a natural slowing effect on revenue growth.

No matter how detailed and thorough the analysis of the underlying factors affecting revenue may be, the revenue forecast will inevitably depart from actual results after just a few months. This level of inherent variability can be massive if a company's sales cycle is quite short, and it has a small backlog of customer orders. In that situation, a company has to create new sales "from scratch" after just a few months, which makes it very difficult to forecast revenue. Conversely, if a company has a massive order backlog that extends beyond the entire forecast period, then the company can probably come fairly close to matching its revenue forecast. However, even in this latter case, there will inevitably be production constraints and delays that impact sales, as will cancelled customer orders – and these issues will build over time to cause an increasing level of variability.

There is no way to deal with the inherent variability of a sales forecast, other than to tailor the period covered by the forecast to the time period over which a company can predict its revenues with a reasonable degree of certainty. Thus, the company in our first scenario may find that it can only create a budget for the next three months, while the company in the second scenario may be able to comfortably prepare a forecast that covers the next two years. An alternative is to intensively review and update the forecast over just the period when sales are relatively predictable, while maintaining a longer-term forecast for which little effort is made to compile a detailed operational budget. Doing so reduces the amount of work that goes into the forecast, while still presenting an approximate view of the company's revenue direction.

## Setting Forecast Boundaries

When a business has no history from which to extrapolate a forecast, it can be useful to set an upper boundary on the maximum amount that can reasonably be achieved, even under the most fortunate of circumstances. The simplest approach is to calculate the size of the total market in which the company has chosen to compete, and then determine the absolute maximum market share that the company can reasonably expect to obtain during the forecast period.

The size of the market can be obtained from industry analysts, or by perusing the market share information that may have been included in the annual and quarterly reports that publicly-held competitors have filed with the Securities and Exchange Commission (available at www.sec.gov). Another option is to peruse the market share reports of industry analysts or industry trade groups. If these sources do not provide sufficient information, a possible option is to buy the credit reports of the primary competitors, and aggregate the self-reported sales information stated in these reports.

The key step in setting a forecast boundary is to arrive at a reasonable projected market share figure. One way to do this is to look for a competitor that is somewhat larger than the company, and determine the amount of its sales. Then divide the competitor's sales by the total industry sales to arrive at a forecast boundary. It usually makes little sense to assume that the company can achieve a notably higher market share in an established market, since it can expect competitors to defend their market shares with aggressive pricing, enhanced customer service, more product features, and so forth.

## Detecting Cresting Sales

When a new product is launched, it may initially appear that unit sales will continue in an uninterrupted, steep angle forever. However, the sales of even the most successful product will begin to ebb at some point, either due to increased competition or because the market has become saturated. From a forecasting perspective, the trick is to detect when sales are beginning to crest, so that sales projections in future periods can be brought back down to earth in a reasonable manner. This is a critical task, since a business might otherwise plan for major new investments to support a product line that will soon experience flat or declining sales.

To create a detection system for cresting sales, it is first necessary to recognize the pattern that a business typically follows to keep expanding its total sales. Initial sales begin with a group of core customers at which the product is specifically targeted. Once the rate of sales to this group begins to decline, sales expansion can be pursued using one or more of the following methods:

- Geographic expansion into similar markets, so that the focus remains on the core customers that were originally targeted – they are now located in places that were not initially addressed.
- Price reductions to address more price-conscious customers, possibly with a reconfigured and somewhat lower-cost product.
- Product reconfigurations to address adjacent markets for which the product was not initially designed. This may result in a substantial product redesign, to the point where the revised product would no longer be attractive to one of the original core customers.

The analyst can then segment sales into each of the preceding classifications, and measure the rate of change in sales for each one. The original markets will likely show cresting sales first, as they become saturated. This information can then be extrapolated to the other sales segments, to predict when sales will crest in each successive market.

---

**EXAMPLE**

Grunge Motor Sports manufactures dirt bikes, including the Caveman XT, Virile XTO, and Potent 4-Stroke. These machines are specifically designed for the performance-oriented young male. The bikes are sold through distributorships, which the company is slowly opening throughout the country.

Grunge's analyst finds that sales in each distributorship follow roughly the same pattern, which is:

|  | Sales Growth Rate % |
|---|---|
| Year 1 | 40% |
| Year 2 | 30% |
| Year 3 | 15% |
| Year 4 | 2% |
| Year 5 | Flat |

This pattern can be applied to each new distributorship in turn to predict when sales will crest.

Grunge then expands its market to introduce a dirt bike targeted at women, called the Petal to the Metal, as well as a dirt bike for middle-aged men, called the Wide Load. These products are positioned outside of the core market group, which results in sales cresting faster – in only three years. This trend is noted in the following table:

|  | Sales Growth Rate % |
|---|---|
| Year 1 | 20% |
| Year 2 | 5% |
| Year 3 | Flat |

The analyst applies this reduced growth rate to all non-core products. The result of these two sales growth rate patterns is a sales forecasting process that can reasonably predict when sales will crest in each segment of the company's markets.

---

When there is a suspicion that sales are cresting, it is more important to pay attention to short-term forecasts, since the rate of growth could change over a relatively short period of time. Conversely, it makes much less sense to place an emphasis on long-term forecasts, since they could show sales continuing to rocket skyward. The concept is illustrated in the following exhibit, where a long-term forecast is sufficiently accurate during the spiraling sales period in Year 1, but must be replaced by a series of shorter-term forecasts from Year 2 onward to provide faster notice of changes as the rate of growth declines.

## Use of Different Forecasts when Sales are Cresting

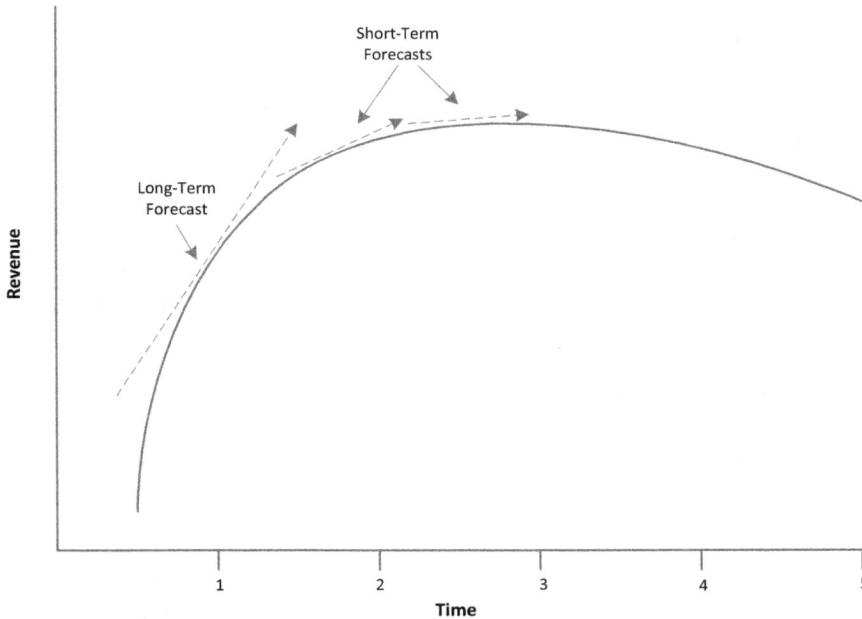

A useful additional concept to consider when monitoring cresting sales is the *saturation level*. This is the point at which all possible buyers have acquired the product or a substitute product, and so will not purchase again, except on a replacement basis. This level can be estimated based on expert opinion and marketing surveys – it is difficult to derive quantitatively without a great deal of expensive investigation. The key point regarding the saturation level is to have an updated estimate of what the saturation level may be, and continually compare this level to actual sales. The comparison is a good indicator of the best case scenario of when sales will crest.

## Evaluation of Forecasts

Once a forecasting method has been selected, one should regularly compare it to actual outcomes in order to determine whether the method is effective. An effective forecast is one that can reliably predict future outcomes with a low level of variation from the actual outcome. If a model is unable to reliably predict outcomes, then it may be causing losses for the organization. For example, a forecast may predict a continuing increase in sales; based on this forecast, a company expands its production into a third shift, hiring production workers and adding more maintenance and supervisory staff.

If the forecasted sales do not materialize, the company has just incurred a loss on the expenses related to the extra shift.

The potential losses that can be triggered by a bad forecast will vary by business. Situations in which a bad forecast has the worst financial effect include the following:

- There is a step costing decision point, where additional fixed costs must be incurred in order to respond to a forecasted sales increase.
- There is a contractual commitment, where the business must commit to buying a certain minimum amount of goods as part of a sales increase.
- There is a fixed asset commitment, where a large investment is required in order to increase sales further.

Conversely, there is much less of an impact if a business has a high unused capacity level, so that it can easily alter its output to match demand.

Monitoring the effectiveness of a forecasting method is a two-step process. First, subtract the forecasted amount from the actual amount, which results in a forecasting error. The following table shows how the forecasting error is calculated.

**Forecasting Error Calculation**

| Forecast Sales | Actual Sales | Forecasting Error |
|----------------|--------------|-------------------|
| $390,000 | $430,000 | -$40,000 |
| 450,000 | 410,000 | +40,000 |
| 420,000 | 425,000 | -5,000 |
| 465,000 | 430,000 | +35,000 |
| 440,000 | 455,000 | -15,000 |
| 470,000 | 485,000 | -15,000 |
| 500,000 | 450,000 | +50,000 |
| 510,000 | 440,000 | +70,000 |
| 490,000 | 435,000 | +55,000 |

The second step is to plot the forecasting error on a chart, to determine when there is a trend of errors bumping up against or breaking through the maximum acceptable upper or lower error limit. A single spike or drop that breaches a maximum or minimum limit might not be cause for alarm, but a continuing trend of breaches in the same direction may be a sufficient reason to search for an alternative forecasting method. A sample trend error chart follows. In the sample chart, the error rate has breached the maximum threshold for the last three periods, which indicates that the underlying forecast model is no longer a reliable indicator of actual activity.

**Trend Error Chart with Min/Max Threshold Levels**

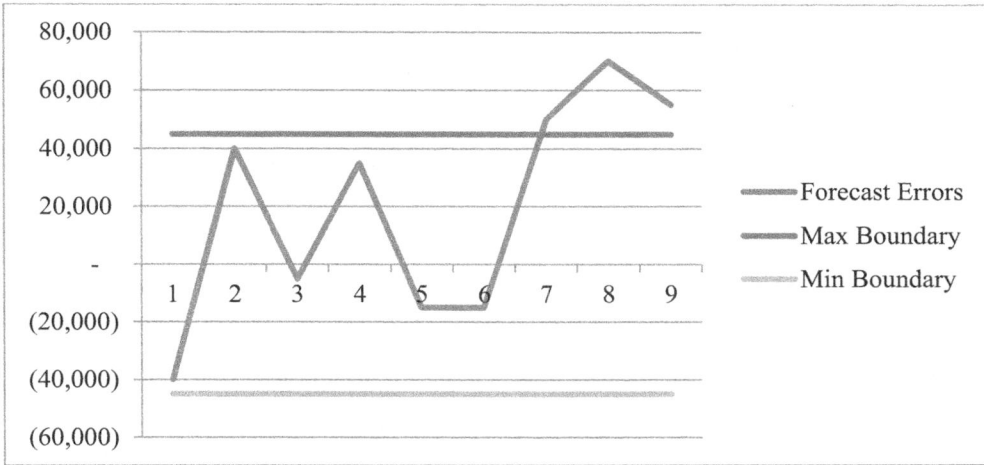

A different type of forecast effectiveness to watch for is the *turning point error*. This is when a forecast does not correctly predict when a trend will reverse. This issue can be critical when production capacity is near its maximum usage level, and any further increases in sales will require a substantial asset investment to support. In such a situation, management needs to know when sales are cresting and will subsequently decline. See the Detecting Cresting Sales section for more information.

A forecast method may have been reviewed, and the conclusion is that it is not effective. Before replacing the method, it may be useful to examine whether other factors are causing the method to produce incorrect results. For example, is the source data sufficiently reliable? It may not be reliable if data is subsequently altered. Also, if there are several sources for the data, does the data vary by source? If so, plug the data from different sources into the forecasting method, and see if the data from one source results in a better forecasting outcome. Finally, is the company using the most recent data? If not, arrange for access to the most recent data, and see if this alters the accuracy of the forecast. If these steps do not improve the forecasting method, it is time to search for an alternative.

## Responsibility for Forecasting

Forecasting is most commonly conducted within the finance and accounting functions, under the supervision of the chief financial officer. However, the sources of this information can come from many parts of a business. For example:

- *Chief executive officer (CEO)*. If the company intends to sell off or shutter certain business segments or acquire other entities, these transactions may have a profound impact on sales. The CEO is in the best position to advise on the probability of these changes to the business.
- *Sales manager*. The sales manager confers with the sales staff to determine the demand for company products at the level of individual customers or

regions. The sales manager will also advise on forecast changes relating to the withdrawal of existing products from the marketplace and their replacement by new products.

- *Contracts manager*. If a company derives some portion of its business from contractual arrangements (such as construction contracts or government services contracts), the contracts manager is the key source of information regarding the remaining funding under each contract, which limits the amount of sales that can be forecasted.

## Summary

Forecasting is the process of estimating a future activity level. Many of the methods available for doing so are based at least in part on historical data. If so, one must remember that historical data do not always indicate what the future will bring. Instead, there may be significant shifts in the industry, product life cycles, or the competitive posture of a business that will cause future results to various significantly from historical results. Given the possibility of such an occurrence, any purely quantitative forecasting method requires an examination and possible modification to reflect the best estimates of these events by those with relevant knowledge.

There are also situations in which no historical data are used to derive a forecast, relying instead on surveys, expert opinions, and similar sources. In these cases, there is a risk that a forecast will be devised that is based to an excessive degree on opinion, which can yield a forecast that is not achievable. This risk can be mitigated by introducing some quantitative rigor, perhaps as simple as comparing historical results to the initial derivation of a forecast that is based on qualitative information.

In short, the best forecast may require both qualitative and quantitative elements. Where a forecast derivation lies along the qualitative – quantitative continuum is up to the forecaster, who needs to balance the cost and effort of forecast compilation with the accuracy of the resulting forecast, as well as the environment in which the business operates.

This chapter has addressed the major forecasting techniques that can be used when estimating future sales. For a comprehensive treatment of how expenses can be projected, see the author's *Budgeting* course, which examines the derivation of costs for all departments of a business.

# Chapter 2
# Financial Modeling

## Introduction

Financial modeling is one of the core job functions of anyone working in the finance and accounting field. It involves the creation of a model that approximates the operating characteristics of a business, which can then be altered to project into the future the possible financial results of the entity. In this chapter, we explore the nature of a financial model, how the modeling process works, and how the model is constructed. We also examine certain aspects of the model in detail, such as depreciation modeling, equity modeling, working capital analysis, and incremental change modeling.

## The Financial Statements

Before we discuss the development of a financial model, it is first necessary to address each of the financial statements that comprise the model. A model contains all three of the financial statements, so that a user can discern the complete impact of a financial event – on profits, financial position, and cash flows. The financial statements include the reports noted in the following subsections.

### The Balance Sheet

A balance sheet (also known as a statement of financial position) presents information about an entity's assets, liabilities, and shareholders' equity, where the compiled result must match this formula, which is called the *accounting equation*:

$$\text{Total assets} = \text{Total liabilities} + \text{Equity}$$

This equation drives the name of the document, where the total of all assets must *balance* the total amount of liabilities and equity. This balancing concept is necessary, since the ownership of an asset can only occur if an organization either pays for it with an obligation (such as a loan) or with the funds invested by shareholders or the ongoing profits of the business (which is equity).

In essence, a balance sheet describes what a business owns, what it owes, and what residual amount net of the first two items is left over for its shareholders. It is used to assess an entity's liquidity and ability to pay its debts.

The balance sheet reports the aggregate effect of transactions as of a specific date. For example, if a balance sheet has been produced as part of a package of financial statements for the month of April, the information contained within the balance sheet is as of April 30, which is the last day of the month. Thus, it essentially represents a snapshot of the financial condition of a business as of a moment in time.

The basic format of a balance sheet is noted in the following exhibit. It contains a header, which describes the name of the entity whose financial information is being reported on, the name of the report, and the date as of which the report was constructed. In the following line items, we have noted how each one adds up into the various subtotals and totals in the document.

## Sample Balance Sheet Format

Lowry Locomotion
Balance Sheet
As of December 31, 20X1

| ASSETS | |
|---|---|
| **Current assets** | |
| Cash | A |
| Investments | B |
| Accounts receivable | C |
| Inventory | D |
| Prepaid expenses | E |
| **Total current assets** | $A + B + C + D + E = F$ |
| | |
| **Non-current assets** | |
| Fixed assets | G |
| Goodwill | H |
| Other assets | I |
| **Total non-current assets** | $G + H + I = J$ |
| | |
| **Total assets** | $\underline{F + J}$ |
| | |
| **LIABILITIES AND EQUITY** | |
| **Current liabilities** | |
| Accounts payable | K |
| Other payables | L |
| Accrued liabilities | M |
| Unearned revenues | N |
| **Total current liabilities** | $K + L + M + N = O$ |
| | |
| **Noncurrent liabilities** | |
| Long-term debt | P |
| Bonds payable | Q |
| **Total noncurrent liabilities** | $P + Q = R$ |
| | |
| **Total liabilities** | $O + R = S$ |
| | |
| **Shareholders' equity** | |
| Common stock | T |
| Preferred stock | U |
| Additional paid-in capital | V |
| Retained earnings | W |
| Treasury stock | X |
| **Total shareholders' equity** | $T + U + V + W + X = Y$ |
| **Total liabilities and shareholders' equity** | $\underline{S + Y}$ |

To see how these calculations are used in a balance sheet, the following example replaces the line item computations with numbers taken from the general ledger of a business.

## Sample Balance Sheet with Numeric Presentation

Lowry Locomotion
Balance Sheet
As of December 31, 20X1

| | |
|---|---|
| **ASSETS** | |
| **Current assets** | |
| Cash | $45,000 |
| Investments | 80,000 |
| Accounts receivable | 425,000 |
| Inventory | 415,000 |
| Prepaid expenses | 15,000 |
| **Total current assets** | $980,000 |
| | |
| **Non-current assets** | |
| Fixed assets | 800,000 |
| Goodwill | 200,000 |
| Other assets | 20,000 |
| **Total non-current assets** | $1,020,000 |
| | |
| **Total assets** | $2,000,000 |
| | |
| **LIABILITIES AND EQUITY** | |
| **Current liabilities** | |
| Accounts payable | $215,000 |
| Other payables | 30,000 |
| Accrued liabilities | 28,000 |
| Unearned revenues | 12,000 |
| **Total current liabilities** | $285,000 |
| | |
| **Noncurrent liabilities** | |
| Long-term debt | 200,000 |
| Bonds payable | 350,000 |
| **Total noncurrent liabilities** | 550,000 |
| | |
| **Total liabilities** | $835,000 |
| | |
| **Shareholders' equity** | |
| Common stock | 10,000 |
| Preferred stock | 50,000 |
| Additional paid-in capital | 320,000 |
| Retained earnings | 825,000 |
| Treasury stock | -40,000 |
| **Total shareholders' equity** | $1,165,000 |
| **Total liabilities and shareholders' equity** | $2,000,000 |

The line items appearing in the preceding balance sheet example are stated in a particular order, which is derived from a concept called the *order of liquidity*. This refers to the presentation of assets in the balance sheet in the order of the amount of time it would usually take to convert them into cash. Thus, cash is always presented first, followed by investments, then accounts receivable, then inventory, and then fixed assets. Goodwill is listed last.

The approximate amount of time required to convert each type of asset into cash is noted below:

1.  *Cash.* No conversion is needed.
2.  *Investments.* A few days may be required to convert to cash in most cases.
3.  *Accounts receivable.* Will convert to cash in accordance with the company's normal credit terms.
4.  *Inventory.* Could require multiple months to convert to cash, depending on turnover levels and the proportion of inventory items for which there is not a ready resale market.
5.  *Fixed assets.* Conversion to cash depends entirely on the presence of an active after-market for these items.
6.  *Goodwill.* This can only be converted to cash upon the sale of the business for an adequate price.

In short, the order of liquidity concept results in a logical sort sequence for the assets listed in the balance sheet. The same concept applies to the liabilities section of the balance sheet, where those obligations most likely to be paid off first are listed first.

**The Income Statement**

The income statement contains the results of an organization's operations for a specific period of time, showing revenues and expenses and the resulting profit or loss. The typical period covered by an income statement is for a month, quarter, or year, though it could cover just a few days.

An income statement is used to measure the ability of an organization to achieve sales, and its efficiency in servicing customers. If a business does well in both respects, then it earns a profit. A profit is the amount by which sales exceed expenses. Instead, if expenses exceed sales, then the entity generates a loss. The cumulative amount of this profit or loss, net of any dividends paid to investors, appears in the retained earnings line item in the balance sheet.

The basic format of an income statement is noted in the following exhibit. It contains a header, which describes the name of the entity whose financial information is being reported on, the name of the report, and the date range for which information is being presented. In the following line items, we have noted how each one adds up into the various subtotals and totals in the document. The flow of information in the statement is to begin at the top with sales, subtract out expenses directly related to sales, then subtract all other expenses to arrive at before-tax income, and then subtract income taxes to arrive at the net income figure.

## Sample Income Statement Format

Laid Back Corporation
Income Statement
For the month ended December 31, 20X1

| Net sales | A |
|---|---|
| Cost of goods sold | B |
| Gross margin | A – B = C |
| | |
| Operating expenses | |
| Advertising | D |
| Depreciation | E |
| Rent | F |
| Payroll taxes | G |
| Salaries and wages | H |
| Supplies | I |
| Travel and entertainment | J |
| Total operating expenses | D + E + F + G + H + I + J = K |
| | |
| Other income | L |
| Total income before taxes | C – K + L = M |
| Income taxes | N |
| | |
| Net income | M - N |

To see how these calculations are used in an income statement, the following example replaces the line item computations with numbers taken from the general ledger of a business.

## Sample Income Statement with Numeric Presentation

Laid Back Corporation
Income Statement
For the month ended December 31, 20X1

| | |
|---|---:|
| Net sales | $1,000,000 |
| Cost of goods sold | 480,000 |
| Gross margin | $520,000 |
| | |
| Operating expenses | |
| Advertising | 10,000 |
| Depreciation | 8,000 |
| Rent | 32,000 |
| Payroll taxes | 25,000 |
| Salaries and wages | 359,000 |
| Supplies | 5,000 |
| Travel and entertainment | 11,000 |
| Total operating expenses | $450,000 |
| | |
| Other income | 10,000 |
| Total income before taxes | $80,000 |
| Income taxes | 30,000 |
| | |
| Net income | $50,000 |

In short, the balance sheet provides a point-in-time picture of a business, while the income statement provides a report card on its results in between these point-in-time snapshots.

## The Statement of Cash Flows

The statement of cash flows is used to identify the different types of cash payments made by a business to third parties (cash outflows), as well as payments made to a business by third parties (cash inflows). Though less frequently used than the balance sheet and income statement, this additional report provides valuable information about the cash status of a business.

This statement is needed, because the information in the income statement does not exactly correspond to cash flows. Instead, an accrual-basis income statement may record revenues and expenses for which cash flows have not yet occurred. In addition, there is no information in the income statement regarding the cash required to support investments in receivables, fixed assets, inventory, and other assets, nor is there any information about cash flows related to the sale of stock, obtaining or paying back loans, and similar matters.

The basic format of a statement of cash flows is noted in the following exhibit. It contains a header, which describes the name of the entity whose financial information is being reported on, the name of the report, and the date range for which information is being presented. In the following line items, we have noted how each one adds up into the various subtotals and totals in the document. The flow of information in the statement is to begin with a derivation of cash flows generated by the operations of a business, followed by the cash flows associated with investing activities and financing activities, which results in a net change in cash for the period. Cash flows are separated into the operating, investing, and financing activities classifications in order to give the reader more information about how cash is generated and used.

### Sample Statement of Cash Flows Format

Newton Enterprises
Statement of Cash Flows
For the year ended 12/31/20X1

| | | |
|---|---|---|
| **Cash flows from operating activities** | | |
| Net income | | A |
| Adjustments for: | | |
| Depreciation and amortization | B | |
| Provision for losses on accounts receivable | C | |
| Gain/loss on sale of assets | D | |
| | | $B + C + D = E$ |
| Increase/decrease in accounts receivables | F | |
| Increase/decrease in inventories | G | |
| Increase/decrease in trade payables | H | |
| | | $F + G + H = I$ |
| | | |
| Cash generated from/used in operations | | $A + E + I = J$ |
| | | |
| **Cash flows from investing activities** | | |
| Purchase of fixed assets | K | |
| Proceeds from sale of equipment | L | |
| Net cash generated from/used in investing activities | | $K + L = M$ |
| | | |
| **Cash flows from financing activities** | | |
| Proceeds from issuance of common stock | N | |
| Proceeds from issuance of long-term debt | O | |
| Dividends paid | P | |
| Net cash generated from/used in financing activities | | $N + O + P = Q$ |
| | | |
| Net increase/decrease in cash and cash equivalents | | $J + M + Q = R$ |
| Cash and cash equivalents at beginning of period | | $\underline{S}$ |
| Cash and cash equivalents at end of period | | $\underline{R + S}$ |

To see how these calculations are used in a statement of cash flows, the following example replaces the line item computations with numbers taken from the general ledger of a business.

## Sample Statement of Cash Flows with Numeric Presentation

Newton Enterprises
Statement of Cash Flows
For the year ended 12/31/20X1

| | | |
|---|---|---|
| **Cash flows from operating activities** | | |
| Net income | | $100,000 |
| Adjustments for: | | |
| Depreciation and amortization | 12,000 | |
| Provision for losses on accounts receivable | 18,000 | |
| Gain on sale of assets | -10,000 | |
| | | 20,000 |
| Increase in accounts receivables | -80,000 | |
| Decrease in inventories | 30,000 | |
| Decrease in accounts payable | -16,000 | |
| | | -66,000 |
| Cash generated from operations | | 54,000 |
| **Cash flows from investing activities** | | |
| Purchase of fixed assets | -80,000 | |
| Proceeds from sale of equipment | 24,000 | |
| Net cash used in investing activities | | -56,000 |
| **Cash flows from financing activities** | | |
| Proceeds from issuance of common stock | 120,000 | |
| Proceeds from issuance of long-term debt | 57,000 | |
| Dividends paid | -32,000 | |
| Cash generated from financing activities | | 145,000 |
| Net increase in cash and cash equivalents | | 143,000 |
| Cash and cash equivalents at beginning of period | | 230,000 |
| Cash and cash equivalents at end of period | | $373,000 |

Some elements of the statement of cash flows are derived from the other financial statements. The net income figure comes from the income statement, along with several of the net income adjustment items. The cash balances at the bottom of the report are taken from the balance sheet, while the increases and decreases in the various assets and liabilities are derived by calculating the differences between the line items in the most recent balance sheet and the same line items in the balance sheet pertaining to the end of the immediately preceding reporting period. For example, the change in accounts receivable noted in the statement of cash flows is derived by calculating the difference in the accounts receivable line items in the last two balance sheets.

## Interactions between the Financial Statements

When a business transaction is recorded in the accounting records, it may impact several of the financial statements at the same time. In this section, we describe a number of these interactions. The intent is to point out how someone reading the financial statements can see how information flows through and is represented in the balance sheet, income statement, and statement of cash flows. Key interactions are as follows:

- *Sales on credit*. When sales are made on credit, the amount appears as both a sale in the income statement and an increase in accounts receivable in the balance sheet. If goods are sold, then this also reduces the inventory line item in the balance sheet by an amount that appears in the cost of goods sold in the income statement.
- *Cash receipts*. When cash is received from a customer in payment of an invoice, this reduces the accounts receivable balance and increases the amount of cash, both of which are located in the balance sheet. This also appears within the operating activities section of the statement of cash flows, since it impacts cash.
- *Buy inventory on credit*. When merchandise and raw materials are acquired from suppliers on credit, the amount appears as both an increase in the inventory and accounts payable line items, which are located on opposite sides of the balance sheet.
- *Receive expenses invoice*. When an invoice is received from a supplier for goods or services that are consumed at once, the amount appears as an expense in the income statement and an increase in the accounts payable liability in the balance sheet.
- *Pay suppliers*. When an invoice is paid, this reduces both the cash and accounts payable line items, which are located on opposite sides of the balance sheet. This also appears within the operating activities section of the statement of cash flows, since it impacts cash.
- *Sell shares*. When cash is received from investors when they buy shares from a business, this increases both the cash balance and the amount of shareholders' equity; these line items are located on opposite sides of the balance sheet. This also appears within the financing activities section of the statement of cash flows, since it impacts cash.
- *Acquire debt*. When cash is received from a lender under the terms of a loan, this increases both the cash and debt liability line items, which are located on opposite sides of the balance sheet. This also appears within the financing activities section of the statement of cash flows, since it impacts cash.

It is useful to consider the preceding interactions when developing a financial model that integrates all of the financial statements.

## The Nature of Financial Modeling

A financial model is a projected representation of the financial results, financial position, and cash flows of an organization. Several variations on this model may be used, which alter key aspects of how an organization is operated, such as an increased product price, altered customer payment terms, and the sale of certain fixed assets. By examining variations on the most likely outcome, managers can bolster their decision-making processes.

Financial models usually share a common set of characteristics, which are as follows:

- *Historical basis*. Projected financial information is derived from the relationships in an organization's historical financial statements. For example, if the most recent financials revealed that accounts receivable turned over six times per year, this amount is built into the next projected period as the baseline case. This approach is used because the manner in which a business operates only changes slowly over a long period of time.
- *Complete financials*. The best modeling approach is to model the complete set of financial statements. By doing so, one can see the interaction of assets, liabilities, and cash flows with the revenues and expenses stated in the income statement. For example, a large projected increase in sales will trigger a substantial increase in the receivables balance, for which an organization may not have sufficient available funding.
- *Integrated ratio analysis*. Financial models nearly always include a set of ratios that are derived from the information in the models. Ratios are needed to test whether financial projections are valid, by comparing them to ratios derived from historical information. For example, the debt/equity ratio, times interest earned, gross margin percentage, net profit percentage, and days sales outstanding could be used to see if a model is generating results that are comparable to what has been achieved in the past.
- *Sensitivity analysis*. A financial model usually contains a sensitivity analysis section. This section includes fields into which can be input changes to key elements of the model, such as (most commonly) a percentage increase in sales, the number of days sales outstanding in accounts receivable, and the amount of inventory turnover. This section may also include key information drawn from other parts of the model, such as profits, the cash balance, and debt. Having this information adjacent to the input fields makes it easier to see how sensitive an organization's financial situation is to certain changes.
- *Operational information*. A financial model may include operational information that is not found in an organization's financial statements. This information can be tied to the financial information in the model to provide insights into the stability of the model. For example, the number of salespeople can be matched against sales to see if the sales per salesperson is reasonable, based on historical experience.

When creating a financial model, one can choose to exactly replicate the financial statements that a business already uses. However, this can create an excessive level of modeling detail that must then be maintained, and also provides more information than managers probably need. Instead, a streamlined model is typically used that represents the key elements of an entity's financial statements. In some cases, it may not be necessary to replicate the entire set of financial statements. Depending on the decisions being examined, it may only be necessary to create a streamlined model for the income statement of an organization.

## The Financial Modeling Process

The best way to construct a financial model is by following a process that defines the problem for which a solution is needed, after which the model is designed, constructed, and tested. By following this approach, a model can be built that only contains those features needed to support the desired outcome, which improves the cost-effectiveness of the model. The basic modeling process follows these steps:

1. *Define the problem.* Determine the exact nature of the problem to be solved. The intent is to drill down to the key aspect(s) of the issue that require a financial model. If the problem definition is excessively broad, a model may be designed that is too comprehensive. Conversely, all necessary aspects of an issue must be included, so that an all-encompassing answer can be given.

---

**EXAMPLE**

Fireball Flight Services is planning to position a private jet in Dallas, so that its clients in that area can be promised immediate flight availability. The company does not currently have a spare jet for this purpose, and so plans to lease one. The company's financial analyst is asked to develop a financial model that describes the profits or losses to be expected from this arrangement. Reasonable questions for the analyst to ask are:

- What is the expected jet utilization level? Will it vary by month?
- What hourly rate will be charged to users? What is the expected average duration of each flight? Will there be a fuel surcharge to cover unusual price spikes?
- What are the payment terms under which customers pay Fireball?
- What will be the terms under which the jet will be leased?
- What is the expected price of jet fuel during the forecast period? Will this price be hedged? If so, what will be the cost of the hedge?
- What will be the jet storage fees charged by the Dallas airport?
- What will be the cost of the flight crew? Will this cost be fixed, or will there be additional charges associated with flight time?
- What will be the cost to bring in a replacement jet when the primary jet is in use? What is the expected proportion of the time that a replacement jet will be needed?

This extensive list of questions broke down the unit volume and prices associated with sales, both fixed and variable aspects of the jet's cost, the capital required to support receivables (if any) and the cost to finance the jet.

---

2. *Assemble specifications.* Create a list of specifications that the proposed financial model will require, and which address the nature of the problem. Several aspects of these specifications are:

- *Time periods.* What time frame should be covered by the model and how granular should the time periods be? For example, is it necessary to break down projections by month or quarter, or is an annual presentation sufficient?
- *Line item groupings.* To what extent can line items be grouped together? A higher level of aggregation makes for a simpler model, but provides less information.
- *Variables.* What variables should be built into the model that can assist with sensitivity analysis? What types of sensitivity analysis should be conducted?

---

**EXAMPLE**

The preceding list of questions related to Fireball Flight Service's positioning of a jet in Dallas reveals that the bulk of the expense associated with the jet will be fixed. The key issue is the extent to which the jet will be used, which may be seasonal. Consequently, a key specification is to model sales by month and by individual customer, to see if there are any periods in which the cash flows generated from the operation cannot cover fixed costs. This also means that a statement of cash flows must be generated, along with the usual income statement. Further, the model must be able to show multiple variations on the amount of jet utilization.

An additional issue is that customers will not be charged a fuel surcharge, but that the cost of fuel can be contained with a hedging program. The cost of the hedging must be included in the model.

A final issue is that a replacement jet will be positioned in Dallas when the primary jet is away servicing customers. The model must be able to determine changes in profitability, based on the percentage of time that a replacement jet is maintained on-site.

Key variables should be listed on a single page of the model, along with a summary of profitability and net cash flows by month, so that the impact of changes in the variables can be easily noted.

---

3. *Build the model.* Create an outline of the financial model that segregates the documentation, variables, data entry fields, calculations, and outputs. Then fill in the outline with the actual model. Include automated audit checks in the model. A number of design principles related to the construction of financial models are noted later in the Model Risk section.
4. *Test the model.* Examine the model for errors, including the use of sample data and testing of the outputs against expected results. Also, isolate each input in turn and make an adjustment to it, to see if the output from the model changes in an expected manner.

The preceding steps may appear to generate a large amount of planning overhead. However, these steps prevent a financial model from generating non-useful or incorrect information, which could have a massively higher cost to a business.

## Key Inputs to the Financial Model

Several inputs are especially useful in the design of a financial model, for they can have a significant impact on the model's outcome. One must be especially careful to verify the historical underpinnings of the following inputs, or else the model will be more likely to produce incorrect results:

- *Profitability percentages*. The gross profit, operating profit, and net profit percentages incorporated into the model should approximate the historical percentages experienced by the entity. It is unwise to model for higher profitability percentages, unless there are identifiable cost reductions that will cause the higher profits.
- *Working capital turnover*. The model should approximately match the historical turnover figures for accounts receivable, inventory, and accounts payable. Assuming an excessively favorable turnover level in one or more of these elements of working capital is one of the most common modeling errors, resulting in a lower investment in assets than is really the case.
- *Debt levels*. The exact due dates of all existing debt must be clarified in the model. If repayments are not noted in the model or are stated incorrectly, then projected cash flows may be thrown off to a considerable extent.
- *Depreciation termination*. Depreciation expenses are typically loaded into a financial model under the assumption of a steady rate of depreciation from period to period. In reality, the depreciation on existing assets will likely decline, as assets become fully depreciated. If not properly set up within the model, there will be an excessive amount of depreciation associated with pre-existing assets.
- *Investment returns*. If an organization has a large amount of investable cash, the presumed return on the investment of those funds could have a major impact on a financial model. Consequently, it makes sense to determine the historical return on invested funds and carry it forward into the model, perhaps with some modest modification.

Other inputs to the financial model do not require historical verification, since they represent best estimates of what conditions will be like during the period covered by the model. Several of these inputs are:

- *Inflation rate*. The projected inflation rate can be modeled at a gross level, or perhaps more accurately as it relates to different aspects of the model. For example, there may be one inflation rate for the prices charged by the company (which may be limited by competitive positions or contractual arrangements), while there is another inflation rate for the cost of goods sold and yet another rate for compensation costs.

- *Growth rate.* A central question in any financial model is the projected rate of growth (or decline) in a company's sales. While some hint of this trend can be discerned from historical information, there are any number of discrete events that are not included in the historical data but which may strongly impact the growth rate, such as changes in consumer preferences, the entry of new competitors into the market, and changes in technology. It may be necessary to apply several different growth rates to the model, if growth is expected to vary by product line or subsidiary.

## Structure of the Financial Model

When a financial model is built, it should ideally contain an interactive set of financial statements, so that changes made to one statement will automatically ripple through the other two statements. For example, the purchase of a fixed asset will reduce the cash balance in the balance sheet while also increasing the depreciation expense in the income statement and creating a cash outflow in the statement of cash flows.

### Variables Section

The variables used in a financial model should be listed first, since this information will be frequently referenced. The variables section is displayed in a matrix, where each related group of variables is stated down the left side of the page. The unit of measure (needed to prevent confusion) for each of the variables is listed in the immediately adjacent column, followed by a column containing the actual variables for the immediately preceding year; this information is used as a baseline against which the variables for the forecast periods can be compared. Finally, there are columns for the forecast periods furthest to the right; these are data entry fields that interact with the information elsewhere in the model. At the bottom of this section are key outputs from the model, which act as a feedback loop for the model designer, to see if the outcomes are reasonable.

An example of the variables section appears in the following exhibit.

## Sample Variables Section

| Variable | Unit of Measure | Last Year | Year 1 | Year 2 |
|---|---|---|---|---|
| **Sales** | | | | |
| Pricing change | % | -- | 1.0 | 2.3 |
| Unit volume change | % | -- | 3.2 | 3.7 |
| | | | | |
| **Expenses** | | | | |
| Cost of goods sold / Sales | % | 42.7 | 41.9 | 41.6 |
| Compensation change | % | -- | 3.0 | 3.0 |
| Other expenses change | % | -- | 2.5 | 2.2 |
| Depreciation rate | % | 14.2 | 13.7 | 13.3 |
| Income tax rate | % | 26.7 | 37.5 | 37.5 |
| | | | | |
| **Financing** | | | | |
| Investment return | % | 2.0 | 2.5 | 2.5 |
| Debt interest rate | % | 8.4 | 7.8 | 7.6 |
| | | | | |
| **Working Capital** | | | | |
| Receivable turnover | Days | 46 | 45 | 44 |
| Inventory turnover | Days | 62 | 60 | 55 |
| Payable turnover | Days | 31 | 32 | 33 |
| | | | | |
| **Key Outputs** | | | | |
| Sales (000s) | $ | 37,050 | 38,597 | 40,988 |
| Gross margin | % | 57.3 | 58.1 | 58.4 |
| Net profit | % | 0.2 | 1.3 | 2.7 |
| Ending cash (000s) | $ | 1,800 | 1,430 | 1,150 |
| Ending debt (000s) | $ | 1,920 | 2,300 | 2,500 |

The information in the variables section illustrates a common problem, which is that financial models typically err on the side of optimism. The variables consistently show increases in revenue, reductions in expenses, and improved returns, as well as a reduced level of working capital. It is quite unlikely that improvements will be generated in *all* of these areas. Instead, one should adopt a more reasonable view of what will happen in the future, which is more likely to involve improvements in some areas and worse results in others.

The next section of the model is the income statement, for which the layout mimics the variables section. An example of the income statement section appears in the following exhibit. In the exhibit, the variables noted in the preceding exhibit are incorporated into the presented numbers. For example, the expected 1% pricing change for Year 1 appears in the income statement as an increase from a $741 unit price in the last year to a $748 unit price in the projected Year 1. Of particular interest in the income statement model is that depreciation is listed as a separate line item. It could have been included in the cost of goods sold and other expenses line items, but it is compiled separately because it is a non-cash expense, and will be needed later in the compilation of the statement of cash flows. Also, note that the interest income and interest expense line items are compiled from a combination of the investment return and debt interest rate stated in the variables section and the ending cash and ending debt balances stated in the balance sheet.

## Sample Income Statement Section

| Line Item | Unit of Measure | Last Year | Year 1 | Year 2 |
|---|---|---|---|---|
| **Sales** | | | | |
| Unit price | $ | 741 | 748 | 766 |
| Unit volume | eaches | 50,000 | 51,600 | 53,509 |
| Net sales (000s) | $ | 37,050 | 38,597 | 40,988 |
| | | | | |
| Cost of goods sold (000s) | $ | 15,840 | 16,172 | 17,051 |
| **Gross margin** | $ | 21,210 | 22,425 | 23,937 |
| | | | | |
| **Administrative Expenses** | | | | |
| Compensation expense (000s) | $ | 11,700 | 12,051 | 12,413 |
| Other expenses (000s) | $ | 7,900 | 8,098 | 8,276 |
| Depreciation (000s) | $ | 1,400 | 1,350 | 1,300 |
| Total administrative (000s) | $ | 21,000 | 21,499 | 21,989 |
| | | | | |
| **Financing Income/Expense** | | | | |
| Interest income (000s) | $ | -36 | -36 | -29 |
| Interest expense (000s) | $ | 161 | 179 | 190 |
| Total financing (000s) | $ | 125 | 143 | 161 |
| | | | | |
| Income before tax (000s) | $ | 85 | 783 | 1,787 |
| Income taxes (000s) | $ | 23 | 294 | 670 |
| Net income after tax (000s) | $ | 62 | 489 | 1,117 |

When deriving the income statement portion of a financial model, a possible option is to set it up in a contribution margin format. Contribution margin is the margin that results when all variable expenses are subtracted from revenue. This means that the gross margin is instead called the contribution margin, and all fixed costs are listed below the contribution margin subtotal. By doing so, the model formulas can be set up so that variable expenses automatically change as a percentage of sales, while fixed expenses do not. This approach also shifts depreciation expense out of the cost of goods. However, the contribution margin layout is not typically used in a company's normal financial statements, so the modeling format may not readily translate over to the financial statements.

The next section of the model is the balance sheet, for which the layout also mimics the variables section. An example of the balance sheet section appears in the following exhibit. The construction of this part of the model involves a number of formulas, which include the following:

- *Accounts receivable.* This amount is based on the receivable turnover days in the variables section and the sales figure in the income statement. For example, the derivation of the $4,759,000 accounts receivable figure for Year 1 is: $38,597,000 sales × (45 turnover days ÷ 365 days).
- *Inventory.* This amount is based on the inventory turnover days in the variables section and the cost of goods sold figure in the income statement. For example, the derivation of the $2,658,000 inventory figure for Year 1 is: $16,172,000 cost of goods sold × (60 days ÷ 365 days).
- *Accounts payable.* This amount is based on the payable turnover days in the variables section and a combination of the cost of goods sold and other expenses in the income statement. For example, the derivation of the $2,128,000 payables figure for Year 1 is: ($16,172,000 cost of goods sold + $8,098,000 other expenses) × (32 payable days ÷ 365 days).
- *Balance check.* There is a balance check line item at the bottom of the balance sheet, which simply subtracts the total assets figure from the total liabilities and equity figure. If the calculation results in anything other than a zero outcome, there is an error in the model.

## Sample Balance Sheet Section

| (000s) Line Item | Unit of Measure | Last Year | Year 1 | Year 2 |
|---|---|---|---|---|
| **Assets** | | | | |
| Cash and investments | $ | 1,800 | 1,430 | 1,150 |
| Accounts receivable | $ | 4,669 | 4,759 | 4,941 |
| Inventory | $ | 2,728 | 2,658 | 2,569 |
| Fixed assets | $ | 9,859 | 9,854 | 9,774 |
| Other assets | $ | 50 | 55 | 60 |
| Total assets | $ | 19,106 | 18,756 | 18,494 |
| | | | | |
| **Liabilities** | | | | |
| Accounts payable | $ | 1,986 | 2,128 | 2,290 |
| Other liabilities | $ | 282 | 187 | 193 |
| Debt payable | $ | 1,920 | 2,300 | 2,500 |
| Total liabilities | $ | 4,188 | 4,615 | 4,983 |

| Equity | | | | |
|---|---|---|---|---|
| Common stock | $ | 3,000 | 3,000 | 3,000 |
| Retained earnings | $ | 11,918 | 12,407 | 13,524 |
| Less: Dividends paid | $ | -- | -1,266 | -3,013 |
| Total equity | $ | 14,918 | 14,141 | 13,511 |
| | | | | |
| Total liabilities and equity | $ | 19,106 | 18,756 | 18,494 |
| Balance check | | 0 | 0 | 0 |

We noted earlier that the universally optimistic assumptions in the variables section may not be realistic. These assumptions resulted in a steep increase in profits in the income statement. In addition, they triggered a decline in working capital that appears in the balance sheet, which the owners plan to take advantage of by voting themselves large dividend payments in each of the next two years. If the optimistic variables are not realized, all of the dividend payouts can be expected to vanish.

The final section of the model is the statement of cash flows, for which the layout varies somewhat from the variables section. The statement of cash flows is partially derived from information in the prior period, and since there is no information for the year prior to last year, the "Last Year" column has been excluded. An example of the statement of cash flows section appears in the following exhibit.

## Sample Statement of Cash Flows Section

| (000s)<br>Line Item | Unit of<br>Measure | Year 1 | Year 2 |
|---|---|---|---|
| **Cash flows from operating activities** | | | |
| Net income | $ | 489 | 1,117 |
| Adjustment for depreciation | $ | 1,350 | 1,300 |
| | | | |
| Change in accounts receivable | $ | -90 | -182 |
| Change in inventories | $ | 70 | 89 |
| Change in accounts payable | $ | 142 | 162 |
| Cash generated from operations | $ | 1,961 | 2,486 |
| | | | |
| **Cash flows from investing activities** | | | |
| Purchase of fixed assets | $ | -1,065 | -- |
| Proceeds from sale of equipment | $ | -- | 247 |
| Net cash used in investing activities | $ | -1,065 | 247 |
| | | | |
| **Cash flows from financing activities** | | | |
| Dividends paid | $ | -1,266 | -3,013 |
| Cash reduction from financing activities | $ | -1,266 | -3,013 |
| | | | |
| Net reduction in cash and cash equivalents | $ | -370 | -280 |
| Cash and equivalents at beginning of period | $ | 1,800 | 1,430 |
| Cash and equivalents at end of period | $ | 1,430 | 1,150 |

Much of the information in the statement of cash flows is derived from information in the income statement and balance sheet, such as net income, the adjustment for depreciation, and the change in accounts receivable (which is calculated from the ending balances in the last two balance sheets). One must be careful about setting the correct positive or negative sign for the cash flows related to receivables, inventory, and payables. Their explanations are as follows:

- *Accounts receivable.* When there is an increase in accounts receivable from the preceding period, this represents a use of cash, since the company has essentially extended a loan to a customer. Thus, an increase in accounts receivable is treated as a negative cash flow, while a reduction in accounts receivable is considered a positive cash flow (since cash is being returned to the company).
- *Inventory.* When there is an increase in inventory from the preceding period, this represents a use of cash, since the company is investing in additional assets. Thus, an increase in inventory is treated as a negative cash flow, while a reduction in inventory is considered a positive cash flow (since the inventory is being converted into cash).
- *Accounts payable.* When there is an increase in accounts payable from the preceding period, this is essentially a loan from suppliers, and so represents a source of cash. Thus, an increase in accounts payable is treated as a positive cash flow, while a reduction in accounts payable is considered a negative cash flow (since the supplier loan is being paid back).

In the example, we have added additional detail regarding the purchase of fixed assets; in the sample business, an equivalent amount of old assets are assumed to have been dispositioned with only a minimal gain or loss, so there is little impact on the balance sheet.

In the statement of cash flows, the ending cash and cash equivalents figure should match the ending cash figure stated in the balance sheet. If there is a difference, there is an error in the model.

In several following sections, we delve into more detail regarding how various line items in the financial model are created.

## Fixed Asset and Depreciation Modeling

One of the more difficult modeling tasks for some organizations is the line items in the financial model for fixed assets and depreciation. In a services business, the investment in fixed assets may be so small that this is a negligible item. However, when a large fixed asset base is required, this asset can be the central user of cash, while depreciation is one of the largest expenses on the income statement. The following bullet points note the full range of modeling options available:

- *Consistent acquisition assumption.* In a steady-state business with only minor growth, assume that fixed assets are being disposed of and replaced at an approximately steady rate. This means that the assumed fixed asset level remains the same, as should the depreciation expense. However, it is still necessary to estimate the amount of cash invested in the replacement assets, which will be factored into the cash flows from investing activities section of the statement of cash flows.

- *Changing acquisitions assumption.* When a business plans to enact significant increases or decreases in the funding of fixed assets, it is not usually possible to incorporate these changes into a simple formula in the financial model. Instead, it will be necessary to create a sub-schedule that itemizes the larger of these investments or asset reductions. Smaller transactions can be aggregated into an "other assets" line item. Depreciation should also be itemized on this sub-schedule. The following exhibit illustrates the concept.

**Fixed Asset and Depreciation Detail Sub-Schedule**

| (000s) | Year 1 | Year 2 |
|---|---|---|
| **Major asset acquisitions** | | |
| Epic driller machine | $1,000 | |
| Filler router machine | | $3,500 |
| Giga pulse machine | 4,200 | 500 |
| Total major assets | $5,200 | $4,000 |
| Total additional minor asset acquisitions | 240 | 280 |
| Total asset reductions | -370 | -510 |
| **Net change in all fixed assets** | $5,070 | $3,770 |
| Depreciation linked to net asset change | $695 | $501 |

If the format in the preceding exhibit is used, then the model should contain one depreciation expense for the baseline amount of fixed assets, plus another depreciation expense for the incremental change in depreciation listed in the example.

> **Note:** An entity's accounting policies may state that the *mid-month convention* is to be used when calculating depreciation. This convention assumes that an asset is always purchased at mid-month, so that the first-month and last-month depreciation for the asset is always for a half-month. We do not recommend using this convention, since the associated modeling of the depreciation expense becomes excessively complicated.

- *Assets tied to employees.* In some businesses, fixed assets are only acquired if a new employee is hired. For example, it may be necessary to equip an office with furniture, a computer, and software when a software developer is hired. In this case, create a sub-schedule within the module that assumes a certain fixed asset investment when there is a net increase in employees. The following exhibit illustrates the concept.

**Employee-Based Fixed Asset Purchases Sub-Schedule**

|  | Last Year | Year 1 | Year 2 |
|---|---|---|---|
| Net change in employees | 3 | 7 | 11 |
| × Fixed assets per employee | $5,000 | $5,200 | $5,200 |
| = Net fixed asset gain | $15,000 | $36,400 | $57,200 |

Another aspect of depreciation that must be included in the financial model is accumulated depreciation, which has a credit (negative) balance. This account contains the cumulative amount of depreciation expense from all prior periods and the current periods. Accumulated depreciation is paired with the fixed assets account to provide a net fixed assets balance on the balance sheet. Accumulated depreciation is a relatively simple calculation in the financial model; it is:

Preceding year accumulated depreciation + Current year depreciation

= Projected accumulated depreciation

Thus, it can only be derived if the ending actual accumulated depreciation figure for the last period is provided.

## Other Assets Modeling

The other assets line item in the balance sheet is a catchall for a number of small accounts, such as prepaid assets and employee advances. The amount in this account is usually so small that it is considered immaterial. If so, the easiest modeling approach is to carry forward the existing balance into the projected periods, without making any changes.

If the balance in other assets *is* significant, it may be necessary to examine the historical data to see if there has always been a large account balance, or if the ending balance is an anomaly. If the company has routinely maintained a large balance in this line item, it is best to assume that the balance will continue through the modeling period. A further adjustment is to potentially maintain an other assets balance that is a percentage of sales, in order to reflect changes in company activity.

If the company has a large recent balance in this line item, but has not historically maintained such a large position, it may be acceptable to gradually draw down the balance to a lower level that more closely adheres to the long-term balance.

## Debt Payable Modeling

The amount of debt payable can be included in a financial model if there are only a few debt instruments and the repayment schedule is consistent through the forecast period. However, if there are a larger number of loans and bonds, then it may be necessary to construct a sub-schedule that feeds into the debt payable line item. This sub-schedule should note the dates and amounts of each debt, for which the total appears in the balance sheet model. The repayment information is also used in the cash flows from financing activities section of the statement of cash flows. The following exhibit illustrates the concept.

### Debt Payable Sub-Schedule

| (000s) | Year 1 | Year 2 |
|---|---|---|
| **Ending Debt Balances** | | |
| Fifth Bank loan | $2,500 | $1,500 |
| Wilkerson Bank loan | 900 | 450 |
| Series A Bond | 10,000 | 0 |
| Total ending debt balances | $13,400 | $1,950 |
| | | |
| **Debt Payments** | | |
| Fifth Bank loan | $1,000 | $1,000 |
| Wilkerson Bank loan | 450 | 450 |
| Series A Bond | 0 | 10,000 |
| Total debt payments | $1,450 | $11,450 |

A further complication arises if a bond is callable. The issuer can buy back these bonds early, subject to whatever conditions are included in the bond agreement. Calling a bond usually occurs when the market rate of interest declines below the rate currently being paid on a bond. Since interest rates are not especially predictable, it is generally unwise to include a bond repurchase event in a financial model, unless the repurchase is already being actively planned.

## Equity Modeling

The only calculation in the equity section of the balance sheet model is for the retained earnings line item. This is the beginning retained earnings balance, plus or minus any gains or losses incurred in the forecast period, minus any dividends paid. Therefore, the beginning retained earnings balance from the last actual period must be included in the model as an input.

The common stock line item does not change unless there is a plan to sell more shares, so this balance is typically carried forward through all forecast periods. Any dividend payments are manually added to the model after running an iteration of the model to ensure that there will be sufficient cash to fund the dividends.

## Balancing the Model

Once all of the inputs have been made to the financial model, the asset side of the balance sheet will not yet match the liabilities and equity side of the balance sheet. This is because estimates, formulas, and "hard coded" numbers have been entered into the model from a variety of sources, without regard to how this information will "play together" in the balance sheet. We must now make an adjustment to the model (a plug) to balance both sides of the balance sheet.

The amount of the plug is noted at the bottom of the balance sheet model, where we have inserted a balance check (see the earlier Sample Balance Sheet Section exhibit). Depending on the sign of the balance check, we must either increase the amount in the cash and investments line item on the asset side, or the amount in the short-term debt line item (not listed in that exhibit) on the liability side. If there are multiple periods being forecasted in the model, the plug may even switch between the two sides if the sign of the number in the balance check changes from period to period.

We use the cash and investments line item to plug the asset side, because this line item is considered a residual account into which excess funds flow if they are not needed for operational or other financing purposes. Similarly, the short-term debt line item is used to plug the liability side, because this line item is considered to be a line of credit that covers any residual obligations generated by the model.

An additional complication arises if the plug creates a balance in the short-term debt line item, which is that an interest expense calculation must be made on this balance. The outcome will reduce net income, which in turn reduces retained earnings, which in turn will alter the amount of the plug. This means that several iterations of the model may be required to balance the balance sheet, as the interest expense changes in response to each alteration in the short-term debt balance. See the Microsoft Excel Modeling chapter to see how these iterations can be automated.

## Covenant Monitoring

A useful addition to a financial model is a block of information that shows required debt covenants and how the business will perform against these covenants during the forecast periods. A debt covenant is part of the debt agreement, and sets forth limitations on organization activities, financial activities, or financial position that must be met; otherwise, a lender can call its loan.

If a financial model indicates that a covenant will likely be breached, the model can then be recast with different assumptions (such as reduced spending) to arrive at a solution in which the covenants will not be breached. A sample of the information block that can be included in the model appears in the following exhibit.

**Sample Covenant Compliance Block**

| (000s) | Covenant Requirement | Year 1 | Year 2 |
|---|---|---|---|
| Dividend payments | None allowed | True | False |
| Profitability (net of income tax) | Over 5% | 6.5% | 4.3% |
| Debt-equity ratio | Maximum 0.5:1 | 0.4:1 | 0.6:1 |

In the exhibit, the company is in compliance in all respects in Year 1, but fails all tests in Year 2. To maintain compliance in Year 2, the organization would have to cancel the planned dividend payment, which might correct the declining debt-equity ratio while also boosting profitability.

## Working Capital Projections for a Growing Business

When a business has experienced flat sales for a long time, management might not consider working capital to be an issue at all. The firm's receivables, inventory, and payables levels are probably fairly consistent over time. However, the situation is entirely different when sales are growing at a rapid rate. In this case, there is likely to be a certain amount of working capital that the business needs to invest in sales, so as sales increase, so too does the need to fund a proportionately increasing amount of working capital.

As a business expands over time, it is possible to use a ratio to estimate whether the amount of working capital now being used is appropriate. We do this by assuming that the historical ratio of working capital to sales represents a reasonable proportion, and then rolling this ratio forward to the current period to see how it compares to the current proportion. If the current proportion has declined, this represents a reduction in the amount of working capital needed to support sales, and vice versa. To derive the working capital roll forward measurement, follow these steps:

1. Calculate the percentage change in revenue from the baseline period to the current period
2. Multiply this percentage change by the working capital figure for the baseline period
3. Subtract the result from the working capital figure for the current period

The working capital roll forward formula is:

$$\text{Current period working capital} - (\text{Baseline period ending working capital}$$
$$\times (1 + \text{percent change in revenue from baseline period}))$$

$$= \text{Working capital roll forward}$$

This measurement is most useful when a company is comparing results between periods that have not been modified by alterations to the business plan, such as changes in price points, expansions into new geographic regions, and so forth. Such changes may alter the amount of working capital that must be maintained, rendering a comparison to working capital in a prior period less applicable to the current circumstances.

---

**EXAMPLE**

Quest Adventure Gear has been expanding rapidly in its core market of rugged travel equipment. In the immediately preceding year, the company required $1,200,000 of working capital to support sales of $5,000,000. In the current year, sales increased by 20%, to $6,000,000, while working capital increased to $1,680,000. The working capital roll forward for the current year is calculated as follows:

$1,680,000 Current period working capital – ($1,200,000 Baseline working capital × 1.2)

$$= \$240,000$$

The ratio reveals that Quest's working capital increased by $240,000 more than expected, based on a proportional comparison to the baseline period. Further investigation reveals that the sales manager granted longer payment terms to a large retailer in exchange for its agreement to sell the Quest line of products.

---

The preceding example illustrates a major issue with rapid increases in sales, which is that gaining market share frequently comes at the price of adding a disproportionate amount of working capital. In the example, sales increased at the expense of allowing longer payment terms to a new customer. As a business tries harder and harder to increase sales, it will likely find that the related working capital cost becomes greater for each additional tranche of sales. The concept is shown in the following chart, where management wants to increase sales at a certain pace, but finds that it can only do so by making decisions at certain points to invest in a greater amount of working capital. The result is not only the typical gradual increase in working capital that roughly matches sales, but also several points at which the working capital investment steps up to a higher level.

**Working Capital Investments to Increase Sales**

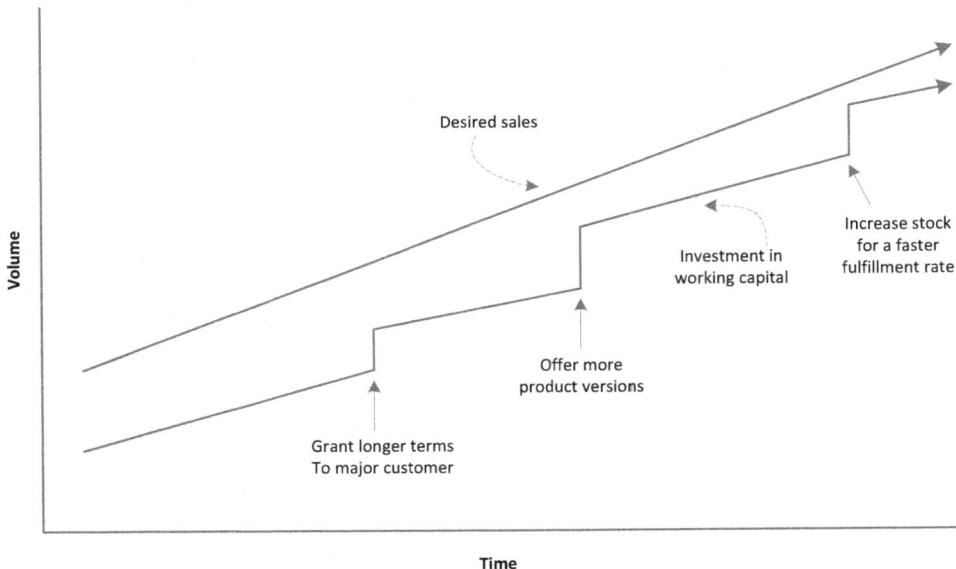

We have established that a large investment in working capital may be needed to fuel rapid sales growth. How is this growth to be funded? The main issue to consider when making this decision is whether the sales increase is expected to be permanent, or if it is a seasonal or one-time event, after which sales will return to a lower level. If sales are expected to be permanent, then funding should come from a long-term debt arrangement or the sale of stock, so that there is a firm source of funding to offset a long-term asset investment. Conversely, if the sales increase is expected to be short-term, then short-term financing solutions may be acceptable, such as a line of credit or receivables financing. The worst situation would be to fund a long-term increase in working capital with a high-cost short-term financing solution, such as receivables financing, since the lender will charge a high interest rate on what will eventually turn into quite a large loan.

In addition, there are two situations in which a business may be able to fund its own growth, which are:

- *High profits*. If a business is generating very high profits on each sale transaction, then the profits generated can fund the requisite working capital investment.
- *Zero working capital*. If an entity has arranged its operations so that there is no working capital investment or only quite a small one, then it can grow without needing to fund any additional working capital.

Many smaller organizations without access to lenders or investors have found that the lack of long-term funding availability to pay for working capital has turned out to be their greatest bottleneck in pursuing rapid sales growth. A common outcome is that they can only grow at a modest clip, plowing profits back into the business to pay for incremental increases in working capital. This results in a slow rate of increase in sales over a long period of time.

As working capital projections pertain to a financial model, the key point is to pay attention to the derived amount of working capital noted in the model, to see if it accurately reflects how management intends to acquire additional sales.

## Working Capital for a Declining Business

The issues just noted for a business with increasing sales are exactly reversed when sales are declining. In this latter case, accounts receivable are being supported in ever-decreasing amounts, while inventory is not being replenished as rapidly as used to be the case. In these situations, there is a one-time increase in cash being spun off from working capital as receivable and inventory levels decrease.

This situation can result in an unexpected cash windfall for an organization that had not anticipated the results of a working capital liquidation, and especially when sales are in a steep decline. As long as management also reduces its outlays for all supporting administrative and other costs as sales decline, it should be possible to accumulate a large amount of cash. When planned for properly through the financial model, this surge in cash can be used to fund new business activities, provide a reserve of cash, and/or a return of funds to investors.

## Sensitivity and Scenario Analysis

When a financial model is constructed, the variables entered into the system may prove to be in error, once the forecasted period actually occurs. The analyst can test for these issues by altering the variables in the model to see how they affect forecasted results. For example, the following analysis shows in the shaded area the particular mix of sales and gross margin percentages that will yield a profit, after accounting for fixed costs. This analysis is easily created with the Data Table tool in Excel, which is described further in the Microsoft Excel Modeling chapter.

### Two-Variable Analysis of Profitability

| | B | C | D Sales | 30% | 32% | 34% | 36% | 38% | 40% | 42% | 44% | 46% |
|---|---|---|---|---|---|---|---|---|---|---|---|---|
| 2 | Profitability Analysis | | | | | | | | | | | |
| 3 | | | $ - | 30% | 32% | 34% | 36% | 38% | 40% | 42% | 44% | 46% |
| 4 | Sales | $ 200,000 | $150,000 | $(35,000) | $(32,000) | $(29,000) | $(26,000) | $(23,000) | $(20,000) | $(17,000) | $(14,000) | $(11,000) |
| 5 | Fixed costs | $ 80,000 | $160,000 | $(32,000) | $(28,800) | $(25,600) | $(22,400) | $(19,200) | $(16,000) | $(12,800) | $ (9,600) | $ (6,400) |
| 6 | Gross margin % | 40% | $170,000 | $(29,000) | $(25,600) | $(22,200) | $(18,800) | $(15,400) | $(12,000) | $ (8,600) | $ (5,200) | $ (1,800) |
| 7 | | | $180,000 | $(26,000) | $(22,400) | $(18,800) | $(15,200) | $(11,600) | $ (8,000) | $ (4,400) | $ (800) | $ 2,800 |
| 8 | | | $190,000 | $(23,000) | $(19,200) | $(15,400) | $(11,600) | $ (7,800) | $ (4,000) | $ (200) | $ 3,600 | $ 7,400 |
| 9 | | | $200,000 | $(20,000) | $(16,000) | $(12,000) | $ (8,000) | $ (4,000) | $ - | $ 4,000 | $ 8,000 | $ 12,000 |
| 10 | | | $210,000 | $(17,000) | $(12,800) | $ (8,600) | $ (4,400) | $ (200) | $ 4,000 | $ 8,200 | $ 12,400 | $ 16,500 |
| 11 | | | $220,000 | $(14,000) | $ (9,600) | $ (5,200) | $ (800) | $ 3,600 | $ 8,000 | $ 12,400 | $ 16,800 | $ 21,200 |
| 12 | | | $230,000 | $(11,000) | $ (6,400) | $ (1,800) | $ 2,800 | $ 7,400 | $ 12,000 | $ 16,600 | $ 21,200 | $ 25,800 |
| 13 | | | $240,000 | $ (8,000) | $ (3,200) | $ 1,600 | $ 6,400 | $ 11,200 | $ 16,000 | $ 20,800 | $ 25,600 | $ 30,400 |

### Variables Sensitivity

A key item to search for when examining the sensitivity of a financial model is which variables cause the largest changes in the model.

**EXAMPLE**

Kelvin Corporation produces mercury-based thermometers. Many of its raw material needs are handled by a supplier that is situated a short distance away, so Kelvin is able to maintain extremely low inventory levels. For this reason, modeled changes in its sales level tend to result in only minor alterations to its projected inventory levels. Thus, the company's inventory is insensitive to changes in sales.

Kelvin's management is debating selling thermometers to "big box" retailers as part of its expansion plan. The typical payment terms demanded by these retailers is 90 days, which is four receivable turns per year. This very low turnover rate means that receivables will increase rapidly if the company sells to this new group of retailers. Thus, the company's receivable levels are sensitive to changes in the sales level.

By altering the variables in the model, one may find that changes in certain variables have a negligible impact on the outcome of the model. If so, it can make sense to remove these variables from the model, so that attention is focused on those remaining variables that trigger significant model changes.

To determine the importance of variables, alter each of the variables in the model in turn by a consistent amount, keeping all other information the same, to determine the impact of each one on the model. Then rank the variables by impact, and review whether those at the bottom of the list (having the least impact) should be eliminated.

How do we measure the impact of a variable on a financial model? Is it the impact on profitability, or perhaps working capital, or even the debt/equity ratio? Impact must be defined by the management team, which creates its definition based on the strategy of the organization. For example, if the primary goal is to maintain a low level of additional funding, then variables will be deemed important if they have an impact on working capital. Or, if the main focus is on tax efficiency, the key variables might be considered those that impact the tax rate (such as sales in a tax-advantaged area). In short, there is no perfect definition for the impact of a variable on a financial model. However, there may be more than one issue that management considers to be crucial, so it may focus on several areas of the financial model over which it wants to monitor changes.

No matter what criteria are considered to be important for the purposes of testing a variable, it is always worthwhile to emphasize those variables that have an outsized impact on the model. For example, if a 10% change in the rate of sales growth causes a 30% increase in the required investment in working capital, management should be informed. Similarly, when a 10% increase in the price of a key commodity triggers a 40% decline in gross margin, this is important.

## Scenario Analysis

Scenario analysis involves the review of multiple alternative outcomes. By engaging in this analysis, one can determine the extent to which various uncertainties can alter a financial model. At a minimum, scenario analysis involves the construction of a base (most likely) case, a worst case, and a best case. Each of these cases may involve a number of changes to the applicable variables. For example, a worst case scenario might include a 20% increase in the cost of a key commodity, a 5% increase in the interest rate on the company's line of credit, a 25% decline in sales when a customer contract is cancelled, and a 5% increase in labor costs caused by a new union contract. All of these factors must be included in the derivation of a comprehensive worst case scenario.

When developing the variables for the worst case scenario, it is important to not simply assign the worst possible outcome for each variable. Similarly, do not assign the *best* outcome for every variable in the best case scenario. Instead, adopt a realistic view of what will happen in either of these scenarios, which may yield mixed results for the variables. For example:

- *Worst case scenario*. A company loses its main customer, which drops sales by 30%. Management immediately lays off staff and eliminates a variety of fixed costs to counteract the expected loss of profits. Since the business will not be able to buy raw materials in such large quantities, it will lose its volume discounts, so its cost of goods sold will increase. Reduced profits will also mean that the company will be in a lower tax bracket, so its tax rate will drop.

- *Best case scenario.* A company gains a massive government contract, which doubles its sales. However, management had to bid an unusually low price to gain the contract, so the cost of goods sold percentage will increase. Also, the company will need to hire additional staff in a tight labor market, so the average wage will increase. The company must also hire contract administrators for the new contract, which increases overhead. Further, increased profits will result in the company moving into a higher tax bracket.

The worst case and best case scenarios are typically designed to encompass situations for which there is a reasonable possibility, not situations that are highly unlikely to occur. Thus, the base case might have a 60% probability of occurrence, while the best and worst case scenarios each have a 20% probability of occurrence.

One way to engage in scenario analysis is to make several copies of a financial model and alter the variables in each one to match the base, worst, or best case scenario. However, this approach runs the risk of having divergent models, if adjustments are made to one model and not copied through to the other models. An alternative approach is the scenario manager tool in Excel, which is described in the Microsoft Excel Modeling chapter.

### Excel Tools

There are several Excel functions available for testing sensitivity and scenarios. See the Scenario Manager, Goal Seek, and Data Table topics in the Microsoft Excel Modeling chapter for more information.

## Incremental Modeling Analysis

When creating a financial model, it is critical to understand when the business is undergoing incremental changes to its business model in order to generate more sales. These changes will inevitably result in altered financial performance that must be recognized in the model. Otherwise, the model will continue to show results along the old trend lines indicated by historical data, when instead the forecast should be substantially different. In particular, consider making incremental changes to the model when the following situations occur:

- *New business segment.* When a new business segment is being added, it may involve different sales growth rates and different working capital turnover levels than are experienced by the rest of the business. This may not initially be a problem, if the activity level of the new segment constitutes a small part of the total sales of the overall organization. However, as the new segment expands, the nature of its operations will begin to skew the outcome of the organization's overall financial situation. To create a more specific model, it may be necessary to create additional line items in the model for each segment. The following example notes how the variables page might be structured for an organization that is comprised of three product segments. The same type of separate treatment could be employed if a company were to take on an unusually large customer that had unusual sales growth rates or receivables turnover.

**Modified Variables Section**

| Variable | Unit of Measure | Last Year | Year 1 | Year 2 |
|---|---|---|---|---|
| **Sales** | | | | |
| Product line A growth rate | % | 1.5 | 1.0 | -0.9 |
| Product line B growth rate | % | 2.9 | 3.0 | 3.0 |
| Product line C growth rate | % | -- | 15.0 | 22.0 |
| | | | | |
| **Expenses** | | | | |
| Cost of goods sold / Sales - A | % | 64.0 | 64.9 | 65.7 |
| Cost of goods sold / Sales - B | % | 51.1 | 51.2 | 51.3 |
| Cost of goods sold / Sales - C | % | -- | 40.5 | 41.0 |
| | | | | |
| **Working Capital** | | | | |
| Receivable turnover - A | Days | 39 | 38 | 37 |
| Receivable turnover - B | Days | 40 | 41 | 42 |
| Receivable turnover - C | Days | -- | 65 | 65 |

In the example variables section, note that product line A is the slowest-growth, highest cost portion of the business. Product line B experiences somewhat better growth, while the new product line C is the targeted high-growth product segment, though at the cost of allowing customers much longer credit terms. If these specifications were to be carried forward into the financial model, the organization would likely find that the model predicts a much higher investment in accounts receivable that is tied to the longer receivable turnover for product line C, which would have been masked if the historical average turnover rate had been used.

- *New product line.* The basic financial model is designed to blend the cost of all products into a single cost of goods sold line item. This approach works well when the cost profile of each product is roughly the same. However, there may be a mix of products with unusually low margins and unusually high margins. If the proportions of these products actually sold vary from their historical proportions, it could cause a major forecast error. In this situation, split the sales and cost of goods sold percentages for the different types of products into separate line items in the model.

- *New sales region.* When a business begins selling in a new sales region, doing so may require a significant boost in distribution costs, especially if a warehousing system must be stocked and maintained in the new region. In addition, the amount of inventory turnover related to the new region may decline, since additional inventory must be stored in that area. This may require the separate specification of a different inventory turnover rate for the new sales region.

- *New country*. When an organization begins operating in a new country, it may be subject to the income taxes charged by the relevant country. This income tax rate may vary from the rate charged by the home country. Consequently, it may be necessary to include in the model an additional line item for each new country's applicable income tax percentage.
- *New debt*. When the total amount of the debt obligation of a business is modest, the interest rate charged on all portions of the debt tends to be at about the same amount. However, when management obtains increasing levels of debt, the risk of nonpayment for the lender goes up, which means that the interest rate charged will also increase. When the debt level reaches these more burdensome levels, there can be quite a spread between the interest rates charged on earlier loans and the most recent loans. If so, consider setting up separate line items in the financial model for each tranche of debt, so that interest rates can be segregated.

The preceding bullet points argue in favor of a more complex financial model. However, this also results in an increased risk of errors, which are detailed in the following Model Risk section. Consequently, only increase the level of model complexity when the outcome clearly warrants the change. Most smaller organizations will find that a basic financial model adequately fulfills their needs.

## Model Risk

A major problem with financial modeling is that models can create errors, which lead to inaccurate results. In particular, the following issues are likely to arise:

- *Incorrect totals*. Certain line items may not have been included in subtotals or totals.
- *Incorrect links*. The information in one financial statement model may incorrectly link into one of the other financial statements, or not at all.
- *Missing information*. Some key line items may not have been included in the model at all.
- *Duplicate information*. Some financial information may have been incorrectly included in several locations within the model, rather than in just one line item.
- *Incorrect formulas*. The calculations used within a model are not correct.

The preceding issues are likely to be exacerbated when a financial model is unusually complex, or if a number of changes have been made to it over a period of time, and especially when multiple people have made changes to the model.

Model risk can be reduced by following several principles when designing a financial model. They are:

- *Simplify.* Keep the model as simple as possible. Resist the temptation to add a multitude of "bells and whistles." It is easier to spot errors in a simple model.
- *Avoid excessive precision.* A model is only a representation of reality, and so will never perfectly reflect the eventual outcome. This means it is not necessary to build inordinate levels of precision into the model. For example, there is no need to create sub-models that will absolutely refine projected facility costs to the last dollar. The elimination of this unnecessary information from a model increases its simplicity, which reduces errors.
- *Simplify calculations.* An unusually lengthy and intricate calculation is more likely to be incorrect. Instead, use the simplest possible calculation or build a calculation through multiple cells so that its logic can be more easily followed.
- *Centralize key values.* A key value such as the tax rate, inflation rate, or inventory turnover rate may be needed in multiple locations within a model. If these values are built into the model in each individual location, there is a high risk that a change will not be enacted for each of these locations. Instead, store all key values in a single central location and reference these values from elsewhere in the model.
- *Centralize calculations.* If a calculation is complex and is used in several parts of a model, store the calculation in just one location and reference it from elsewhere in the model. Doing so allows the user to maintain tight control over changes to the calculation.
- *Use a consistent layout.* Every aspect of a financial model should follow a standard layout in terms of information presented, formulas, time periods used, and subtotals and totals. The standard flow is from left to right and from top to bottom. By rigidly adhering to a consistent layout, model users are less likely to build their own unique adjustments into the model.
- *Employ colors.* Use different colors within the model to highlight different types of cells. For example, a data entry field could be shaded in blue, while a formula field might be shaded in red. These designations are useful for clarifying how a model is to be used.
- *Document the model.* Fully document the reasons for all inputs, so that incorrect information is not entered. Also, add text to the model whenever there are sections for which there may be multiple interpretations, or when the information presented is not clear. Further, note the meaning of any coloration used in the model.
- *Include audit checks.* A number of tests can be added to a model to flag whether certain items are incorrect. For example, does the balance sheet balance? Are fixed assets being depreciated more than their book values? Is the cash balance dropping below zero? These audit checks can be flagged in one central location, so that it is immediately obvious to the user when there is a problem.

- *Lock cells*. Where possible, lock all cells except those intended for data entry use. Doing so eliminates the risk that an adjustment will be incorrectly made to the wrong cell.
- *Validate the model*. Consider adding validation screening to data entry fields, which will warn the user when unusually high or low values are entered.
- *Review the model*. When the results of a financial model are particularly important (such as when the results will be released to an outside party), schedule a review meeting with a person knowledgeable in financial modeling, and walk through the model. Discuss the nature of all calculations, how information flows through the model, and the assumptions used in developing the model. In addition, conduct a review whenever the model is altered.
- *Store copies*. If a model is being routinely updated over time, store a copy of each preceding version. By doing so, one can more easily return to an earlier version if the current version proves to be unreliable.

The preceding design principles will not eliminate model risk, since there is a human element in the creation of models that will always introduce some risk of error. Nonetheless, the risk of error can be reduced.

## Budgeting and Planning Software

It is possible that a financial model *must* be large and complex, perhaps because the underlying business has these characteristics. If so, all of the preceding issues can be avoided by switching to budgeting and planning (B&P) software. B&P software centralizes the storage and use of budgeting information. This system centralizes planning information, reduces data error rates, and makes it easier to model future outcomes.

This software presents a common user interface to all users, and stores all submitted information in a central database. The information in this database is rendered into a financial model by the modeling software. Users cannot adjust the software, other than through adjustments to the various user-specific flags (which are password protected), and so cannot introduce any modeling errors.

When users enter data, the system can be configured to present them with just the information required for their department, possibly along with historical or other information that they can use as a basis for developing their forecast estimates. The system may also allow them to copy forward actual results from prior periods into the data entry fields in the model.

The system can also present users with the pro forma results of their departments (see the next section), based on the information they have entered into the system. This information is useful for adjusting budget information. There may also be boundary warnings, which notify users if they input forecast information that exceeds certain predetermined maximum or minimum values.

A better B&P system contains an integrated workflow management system, which managers can use to monitor who has updated their information, and which requested information has yet to be input into the system.

## Pro Forma Financial Statements

Pro forma financial statements incorporate assumptions or hypothetical conditions regarding past or future events. These statements are useful for presenting possible financial results to outsiders, such as prospective investors. For example, pro forma statements can be constructed that extend an entity's financial statements through the end of its current fiscal year, containing assumptions regarding the final months of the year that have not yet occurred. Similarly, pro forma statements can include the results of a recent acquisition, as though it had occurred earlier, as of the beginning of the year.

Pro forma statements are an ideal use for financial modeling, since a model can be designed to incorporate the assumptions needed to develop and update pro forma statements.

## Responsibility for Modeling

Financial modeling is clearly the responsibility of the financial analyst, since advising management about various financial choices is the core activity of this position. If there is no financial analyst, the role is usually taken on by whoever is responsible for budgeting, since a budget model is similar to a financial model.

The analyst must have an excellent knowledge of electronic spreadsheets, in order to construct and manipulate financial models. One must also understand how the information in the three financial statements interacts.

The information that a financial analyst needs to construct a financial model comes from all parts of a business, with particular emphasis on the following positions:

- *Controller*. The controller constructs the monthly, quarterly, and annual financial statements, and so is the primary source of historical financial information.
- *Sales manager*. The sales manager provides short-term sales estimates, based on the opinions of the sales staff regarding individual customers and sales regions.
- *Marketing manager*. The marketing manager can provide information about the timing of future marketing campaigns, which can be used to estimate sales spikes for certain products.
- *Engineering manager*. The engineering manager can provide information about the release dates of new products, as well as the termination of older products, which can influence the sales forecast.

## Summary

Financial modeling can be an extremely detailed activity. This means that the analyst constructing a model may become so buried in the details that she does not see the larger issues that the model is intended to address. A particular concern is when a model is constructed to only reveal a single outcome, such as a single view of the budget for the upcoming year. A much more likely scenario is that the actual outcome will fall within a certain range, perhaps (for example) with a 20% variance on either side of the amount presented. The analyst must be able to recognize these situations, and use the model to present management with the full range of possible outcomes. Doing so yields a much more comprehensive set of information from which to make a decision.

The most sophisticated modeling in the world will not result in an improvement in management decision making unless it is properly communicated to the recipients of the model. This means there should be a cogent interpretation of the results of the model that explains key assumptions and calculations, as well as unexpected outcomes and why they appear in the model. Where possible, it is useful to personally convey one's findings to recipients, in order to answer any questions they may have and to provide additional details as needed.

# Chapter 3
# Cash Forecasting

## Introduction

It is impossible to manage cash effectively without an accurate cash forecast. The forecast is designed to give management insights into the state of cash inflows and outflows over the next few weeks and months. A well-constructed forecast should give employees sufficient information to ensure that there is enough cash available to meet the ongoing needs of a business on a day-to-day basis. The forecast should be sufficiently reliable so that funds can be invested in somewhat longer-term investments, without being concerned that there will be a sudden need for the cash prior to the maturity dates of the investments.

Clearly, it is imperative to have a cash forecast that is completely reliable. In this chapter, we cover the details of how to create such a forecast, the reliability of the source information used within it, and how to improve the document on an ongoing basis.

## The Cash Forecast

The management team needs to know the amount of cash that will probably be on hand in the near future, in order to make fund raising and investment decisions. This is accomplished with a cash forecast, which should be sufficiently detailed to warn of projected cash shortfalls and excess funds on at least a weekly basis. This section covers the details of how to create and fine-tune a cash forecast.

The cash forecast can be divided into two parts: near-term cash flows that are highly predictable (typically covering a one-month period) and medium-term cash flows that are largely based on revenues that have not yet occurred and supplier invoices that have not yet arrived. The first part of the forecast can be quite accurate, while the second part yields increasingly tenuous results after not much more than a month has passed. It is also possible to create a long-term cash forecast that is essentially a modified version of the company budget, though its utility is relatively low. The following exhibit shows the severity of the decline in accuracy for short-term and medium-term forecasts. In particular, there is an immediate decline in accuracy as soon as the medium-term forecast replaces the short-term forecast, since less reliable information is used in the medium-term forecast.

## Variability of Actual from Forecasted Cash Flow Information

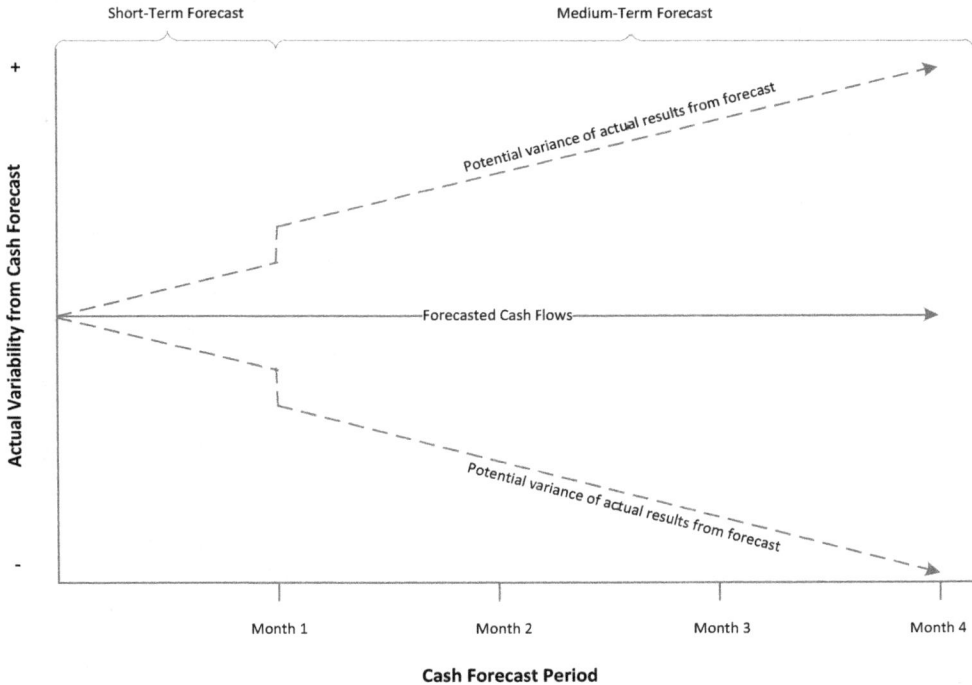

Through the remainder of this section, we will deal separately with how to construct the short-term and medium-term portions of the cash forecast, along with related topics.

### The Short-Term Cash Forecast

The short-term cash forecast is based on a detailed accumulation of information from a variety of sources within the company. The bulk of this information comes from the accounts receivable, accounts payable, and payroll records, though other significant sources are the treasurer (for financing activities), the chief financial officer (for acquisitions information) and even the corporate secretary (for scheduled dividend payments). Since this forecast is based on detailed itemizations of cash inflows and outflows, it is sometimes called the *receipts and disbursements method*.

The forecast needs to be sufficiently detailed to create an accurate cash forecast, but not so detailed that it requires an inordinate amount of labor to update. Consequently, include a detailed analysis of only the *largest* receipts and expenditures, and aggregate all other items. The detailed analysis involves the manual prediction of selected cash receipts and expenditures, while the aggregated results are scheduled based on average dates of receipt and payment (see the comments at the end of this section about the use of averaging).

> **Tip:** Use detailed analysis of cash items in the cash forecast for the 20% of items that comprise 80% of the cash flows, and use aggregation for the remaining 80% of items that comprise 20% of the cash flows.

The following table notes the treatment of the key line items in a cash forecast, including the level of detailed forecasting required.

## Cash Forecast Line Items

| +/- | Line Item | Discussion |
|-----|-----------|------------|
| + | Beginning cash | This is the current cash balance as of the creation date of the cash forecast, or, for subsequent weeks, it is the ending cash balance from the preceding week. Do not include restricted cash in this number, since you may not be able to use it to pay for expenditures. |
| + | Accounts receivable | Do not attempt to duplicate the detail of the aged accounts receivable report in this section of the forecast. However, the largest receivables should be itemized, stating the period in which cash receipt is most likely to occur. All other receivables can be listed in aggregate. |
| + | Other receivables | Only include this line item if there are significant amounts of other receivables (such as customer advances) for which you expect to receive cash within the forecast period. |
| - | Employee compensation | This is possibly the largest expense item, so be especially careful in estimating the amount. It is easiest to base the compensation expense on the amount paid in the preceding period, adjusted for any expected changes. |
| - | Payroll taxes | List this expense separately, since it is common to forget to include it when aggregated into the employee compensation line item. |
| - | Contractor compensation | If there are large payments to subcontractors, list them in one or more line items. |
| - | Key supplier payments | If there are large payments due to specific suppliers, itemize them separately. You may need to change the dates of these payments in the forecast in response to estimated cash positions. |
| - | Large recurring payments | There are usually large ongoing payments, such as rent and medical insurance, which can be itemized on separate lines of the forecast. |

| +/- | Line Item | Discussion |
|---|---|---|
| - | Debt payments | If there are significant principal or interest payments coming due, itemize them in the report. |
| - | Dividend payments | If dividend payments are scheduled, itemize them in the forecast; this tends to be a large expenditure. |
| - | Expense reports | If there are a large number of expense reports in each month, they are probably clustered near month-end. You can usually estimate the amount likely to be submitted. |
| = | Net cash position | This is the total of all the preceding line items. |
| +/- | Financing activities | Add any new debt, which increases cash flow, or the reduction of debt, which decreases cash flow. Also add any investments that mature during the period. |
| | Ending cash | This is the sum of the net cash position line item and the financing activities line item. |

The following example illustrates a cash forecast, using the line items described in the preceding table.

## EXAMPLE

The controller of Suture Corporation constructs the following cash forecast for each week in the month of September.

| +/- | Line Item | Sept. 1-7 | Sept. 8-14 | Sept. 15-22 | Sept. 23-30 |
|---|---|---|---|---|---|
| + | Beginning cash | $50,000 | $30,000 | $2,000 | $0 |
| + | Accounts receivable | | | | |
| + | Alpha Pharmaceuticals | 120,000 | | 60,000 | |
| + | St. Joseph's Burn Center | | 85,000 | | 52,000 |
| + | Third Degree Burn Center | 29,000 | | 109,000 | |
| + | Other major receivables | 160,000 | 25,000 | 48,000 | 60,000 |
| + | Other receivables | 10,000 | | 5,000 | |
| - | Employee compensation | 140,000 | | 145,000 | |
| - | Payroll taxes | 10,000 | | 11,000 | |
| - | Contractor compensation | | | | |
| - | Bryce Contractors | 8,000 | | 8,000 | |
| - | Johnson Contractors | 14,000 | | 12,000 | |
| - | Key supplier payments | | | | |
| - | Chico Biomedical | 100,000 | | 35,000 | |
| - | Stanford Research | 20,000 | 80,000 | 29,000 | 14,000 |
| - | Other suppliers | 35,000 | 40,000 | 30,000 | 48,000 |
| - | Large recurring payments | | | | |
| - | Medical insurance | | | | 43,000 |
| - | Rent | | | | 49,000 |
| - | Debt payments | | 18,000 | | |
| - | Dividend payments | | | 20,000 | |
| - | Expense reports | 12,000 | 0 | 0 | 21,000 |
| = | Net cash position | $30,000 | $2,000 | -$66,000 | -$63,000 |
| +/- | Financing activities | | | 66,000 | 63,000 |
| = | Ending cash | $30,000 | $2,000 | $0 | $0 |

The forecast reveals a cash shortfall beginning in the third week, which will require a cumulative total of $129,000 of additional financing if the company wants to meet its scheduled payment obligations.

The format is designed with the goal of giving sufficient visibility into cash flows to reveal the causes of unusual cash shortfalls or overages, without burying the reader in an excessive amount of detail. To meet this goal, note the use of the "Other receivables" and "Other suppliers" line items in the exhibit. They are used to aggregate smaller projected transactions that do not have a major impact on the forecast, but which would otherwise overwhelm the document with an excessive amount of detail if they were listed individually.

A possible addition to the cash forecast is the use of a *target balance*. This is essentially a "safety stock" of cash that is kept on hand to guard against unexpected cash requirements that were not planned for in the cash forecast. All excess cash above the target balance can be invested, while any shortfalls below the target balance should be funded. If a target balance had been incorporated into the preceding cash forecast example in the amount of $10,000, the amount would have been listed for the week of September 1-7 as a deduction from the ending cash position, leaving $20,000 of cash available for investment purposes.

The model we have outlined in this section requires a weekly update. It only covers a one-month period, so its contents become outdated very quickly. Ideally, time should be blocked out in the department work schedule to complete the forecast at the same time, every week. Unless the business is operating in an extremely tight cash flow environment, we do not recommend daily updates of cash forecasts – the time required to create these forecasts is excessive in comparison to the additional precision gained from the more frequent updates.

---

**Tip:** Do not schedule an update of the cash forecast on a Monday or Friday, since too many of these days involve holidays. Instead, schedule the forecast update on any other business day, thereby increasing the odds of completing a new forecast every week.

---

The very short-term portion of the cash forecast may be subject to some tweaking, usually to delay a few supplier payments to adjust for liquidity problems expected to arise over the next few days. To incorporate these changes into the forecast, use a preliminary draft of the forecast to coordinate changes in the timing of payments with the controller, and then record the delays in the forecast before issuing the final version.

### The Medium-Term Cash Forecast

The medium-term cash forecast extends from the end of the short-term forecast through whatever time period is needed to develop investment and funding strategies. Typically, this means that the medium-term forecast begins one month into the future.

The components of the medium-term forecast are largely comprised of formulas, rather than the specific data inputs used for a short-term forecast. For example, if the sales manager were to contribute estimated revenue figures for each forecasting period, then the model could derive the following additional information:

- *Cash paid for cost of goods sold items.* Can be estimated as a percentage of sales, with a time lag based on the average supplier payment terms.
- *Cash paid for payroll.* Sales activity can be used to estimate changes in production headcount, which in turn can be used to derive payroll payments.

- *Cash receipts from customers.* A standard time lag between the billing date and payment date can be incorporated into the estimation of when cash will be received from customers.

A possibly more precise method for deriving cash paid for cost of goods sold items is based on the presence of a constraint somewhere in the company's production or administrative systems that chokes the flow of orders. If this bottleneck exists, estimate sales based on the capacity of the constraint; at a minimum, do *not* forecast for cash flows derived from sales that exceed the capability of the constraint, since it is impossible for the system to generate these additional amounts.

The concept of a formula-filled cash forecast that automatically generates cash balance information breaks down in some parts of the forecast. In the following areas, it will be necessary to make manual updates to the forecast:

- *Fixed costs.* Some costs are entirely fixed, such as rent, and so will not vary with sales volume. Be aware of any contractually-mandated changes in these costs, and incorporate them into the forecast.
- *Step costs.* If revenues change significantly, the fixed costs just described may have to be altered by substantial amounts. For example, a certain sales level may mandate opening a new production facility. A more common step cost is having to hire an overhead staff position when certain sales levels are reached. Be aware of the activity levels at which these step costs will occur.
- *Seasonal / infrequent costs.* There may be expenditures that only arise at long intervals, such as for the company Christmas party. These amounts are manually added to the forecast.
- *Contractual items.* Both cash inflows and outflows may be linked to contract payments, as may be the case with service contracts. If so, the exact amount and timing of each periodic payment can be transferred from the contract directly into the cash forecast.

The methods used to construct a medium-term cash forecast are inherently less accurate than the much more precise information used to derive a short-term forecast. The problem is that much of the information is derived from the estimated revenue figure, which rapidly declines in accuracy just a few months into the future. Because of this inherent level of inaccuracy, do not extend the forecast over too long a time period. Instead, settle upon a time range that provides useful information for planning purposes. Any additional forecasting beyond that time period will waste staff time to create, and may yield misleading information.

## The Long-Term Cash Forecast

There can also be a long-term cash forecast that extends for an additional one or two years past the end of the medium-term forecast. It can be extremely difficult and time-consuming to develop and maintain a sales forecast for this period, so the most common approach is to instead adapt information from the corporate budget, and update it regularly to coincide with management's best estimates of long-term results.

The cash flows indicated by a long-term cash forecast should be considered only approximate values, so one would be justified in not using it as the basis for any investment activities having specific maturity dates. However, the long-term forecast may be of more use in dealing with projected cash shortfalls. For lack of any better information, this forecast can be used to obtain approximations of how much cash may be needed, and to plan on acquiring debt or selling stock to meet the shortfall.

## The Use of Averages

There can be a temptation to use averages for estimated cash flows in the cash forecast. For example, it may seem reasonable to divide the average cash collections for receivables in a month by four, and then enter the resulting average cash receipts figure in each week of the forecast. This is not a good idea in the short-term portion of the forecast, since there are a number of timing differences that will make actual results differ markedly from average results. The following bullets contain several cash flow issues that can have sharp spikes and declines in comparison to the average:

- The receipt of payment for an unusually large invoice
- The designation of a large invoice as a bad debt
- Once-a-month payments, such as rent and medical insurance
- Sporadic payments, such as for dividends and property taxes

It is particularly dangerous to use averaging to estimate accounts receivable. In many companies, there is a disproportionate amount of invoicing at the end of each month, which means that there is a correspondingly large amount of cash receipts one month later (assuming 30-day payment terms). In short, it is quite common to have billing surges cause payment surges that vary wildly from average cash receipt numbers.

If management were to rely upon an averages-based cash forecast, there would be a high risk of routinely having cash shortfalls and overages. After all, management is responsible for ensuring liquidity *every day*, not just on average. Thus, we strongly recommend against the use of averages when forecasting the larger items in a short-term cash forecast.

The situation is different in a medium-term forecast, since the time period is sufficiently far into the future to make it impossible to predict cash flows with any degree of precision. In this case, one must estimate based on averages, though with three enhancements:

- Insert specific cash flows that are certain, such as contractually-mandated payments or receipts.
- Insert specific cash flows that have historically proven to be reliable. For example, if a customer has proven to be consistent in paying on a certain day of the month, assume that these payments will continue with the same timing.
- It may be possible to substitute actual cash flow information for averages in the least-distant time periods. This is particularly likely for cash outflows, such as payroll, where there is not a significant amount of change in the amount paid from period to period.

## Automated Cash Forecasting

Some accounting software packages include a feature that estimates cash balances in the near future, based on outstanding accounts receivable and accounts payable and when they are supposed to be paid. The feature should be used with caution in cash forecasting, given the following pluses and minuses associated with how they operate:

- *Cash outflow estimates.* The systems can be quite accurate in estimating accounts payable, since they draw upon the mandated payment terms listed in the vendor master file in the accounting system. However, the accounting department must be very good at entering all accounts payable into the system immediately upon receipt, to ensure that these items are properly reflected in the cash forecast.
- *Cash collection estimates.* Cash receipt estimates will necessarily be less accurate, since customers do not always pay in accordance with the payment terms listed in the customer master file. Also, customer accounts payable departments may be irregular in making payments around major holidays, which an automated system does not account for.
- *Available for use information.* Automated cash forecasting systems project cash balances based on the issuance or receipt of payments, which differ from the availability dates of the underlying checks.
- *Undocumented cash outflows.* Many companies have short-term cash outflow requirements related to fixed asset purchases, legal settlements, acquisitions, and so on that are not entered into the accounts payable system until the day when payment is to be made. These payments can unexpectedly alter the results of an automated system by a substantial amount.

> **Tip:** It is easier to automate the cash forecast when suppliers send their invoices directly to the accounts payable department, rather than to their contacts elsewhere in the company, thereby shortening the time required to record the invoices. Better yet, have suppliers submit their invoices through an on-line interface, so that payables are included in the forecasting model as early as possible.

An automated system that relies upon accounts payable to determine cash outflows is probably only accurate through a time period of about two to three weeks. To extend the accuracy of the forecast, consider routing requests for all larger purchases through the purchasing department; doing so allows for the creation of purchase orders that incorporate pricing and delivery dates, which can then be integrated back into the cash forecast. The result should be a cash forecast whose cash outflow information is accurate for a few more weeks into the future.

Given these issues, it would likely be necessary to modify the results provided by an automated cash forecasting system, especially in regard to projected cash receipts from customers. For medium-term forecasts, the detailed cash receipt and disbursement information used by these systems is not available, rendering them much less effective.

## The Reliability of Cash Flow Information

After building cash forecasts for a few months, it will become apparent that certain information is highly reliable, while other types of information vary considerably from expectations. It is useful to identify which types of information are *least* reliable, so that the most time can be spent monitoring them. Highly reliable information can be copied forward into successive versions of the cash forecast with minimal cross-checking. The following bullet points note the reliability of different types of cash flow information:

**Reliability of Cash Flow Information**

| Cash Flow Item | Reliability | Comments |
|---|---|---|
| **Cash Inflows** | | |
| Credit sales | Average | If there are many small invoices, it should be possible to calculate the time periods within which certain proportions of all billed invoices will be paid. The situation is more dire if there are a few large invoices, since reliability is subject to the whims of a few customers. Timing is particularly problematic for payments coming from international customers, since there are more ways in which payments can be held up in transit. |
| Investments | Very high | If an investment has a specific maturity date, the related cash receipt can be scheduled with high confidence. |
| **Cash Outflows** | | |
| Payroll | High | If a company uses a third party payroll supplier, the full amount of the payroll will be extracted from the company's account on a specific date. If payroll is handled in-house and especially with check payments, then the reliability of payments will be high within a period of a few days. |
| Suppliers | High | The payment dates for supplier payments are based on negotiated payment terms, which make the reliability of this information quite high. The reliability can be eroded if there are payment disputes with suppliers that delay payments. |
| Income tax payments | Varies | Quarterly income tax payments can be based on prior year payments, and so are very predictable. However, the final annual payment is based on annual net profits, which may be considerably less predictable. |
| Other tax payments | High | Sales tax remittances are usually compiled several weeks in advance, and can also be predicted as a percentage of sales. |
| Dividends | Very high | The amount and timing of dividends are determined several months in advance by the board of directors. |
| Debt payments | Very high | Debt repayment schedules are usually quite rigidly enforced. The lender may even use an ACH debit to extract debt payments from the company's bank account on specific dates. |

The preceding table points out that the credit sales component of cash inflows can have the most problematic reliability. Thus, this is likely to be the area in which one should focus attention when developing a cash forecast.

## The Impact of Special Events

There are a number of special events that can have a profound (and usually negative) impact on the cash forecast. From the perspective of cash management, it is critical to identify these events and incorporate them into the cash forecast as early as possible. Doing so improves the likelihood that sudden cash shortages can be avoided. Here are several examples of special events that can impact cash flows:

- *Commodity price spikes.* The price of a key commodity suddenly increases, and the company is unable to pass the increase through to its customers. This will cause a significant jump in cash outflows in 30 days, when supplier invoices are due for payment. This will impact the transitional period in the cash forecast between the end of the short-term forecast and the start of the medium-term forecast.
- *Competing product introduction.* A competitor unexpectedly introduces an excellent competing product at a low price point, which immediately drives down the company's market share. This will impact the medium-term cash forecast, as sales drop and cash inflows decline.
- *Supply chain disruption.* A flood destroys a key supplier facility. It will take three months to mitigate the supply chain damage. In the meantime, existing buffer stocks of finished goods will be drawn down and sales will then terminate for all goods containing the parts provided by the supplier. This will not impact the short-range cash forecast, but may trigger a massive decline in cash inflows from customers over the medium term.
- *War.* An insurgency impacts deliveries into a key market in the Middle East, cutting off the company from its distributors. All sales are expected to cease until the insurgency can be put down. This will certainly impact the medium-term forecast, and may even roll into the short-term forecast, if the impacted distributors cannot make payments on outstanding invoices.

These examples of special events all impact the cash forecast to a major extent. It is entirely possible that a business may be subjected to at least one of these events every year or so. Given the reasonable probability of these occurrences, it is of some importance to maintain strong lines of communication with everyone in the company who is most likely to be best informed about these events. This means having ongoing discussions with the purchasing manager to understand changes in the supply chain, as well as with the sales manager to learn firsthand what is happening with the company's products and distribution systems. This enhanced level of communication allows for the more rapid inclusion of special events in the cash forecast.

> **Tip:** Include in the forecasting procedure a requirement to contact the purchasing and sales managers for updates on special events. Otherwise, this investigation will likely be forgotten.

## The Foreign Currency Cash Forecast

The cash forecast is particularly useful when a company deals with large amounts of foreign currency. In these cases, consider maintaining a separate cash forecast for each foreign currency. By doing so, it is much easier to identify possibly excessive exposures to large foreign currency holdings or payment requirements, which may trigger a variety of hedging activities.

> **Tip:** It may be possible to develop a consolidated cash forecasting system that is comprised of separate foreign currency forecasts that roll up into a corporate-level forecast.

## Cash Forecast Reconciliation

No matter how excellent a job may be done in constructing a cash forecast, the result will never exactly match actual results. Either the amount or timing of actual cash inflows and outflows will differ from the prediction. Because of these differences, the people responsible for generating each cash forecast should routinely conduct a forecast reconciliation. The reconciliation should encompass the following activities:

- Investigate items that were expected to occur, but which did not
- Investigate items that were entirely unanticipated, or which were accelerated
- Investigate items that occurred in unanticipated amounts

The result can be a formal reconciliation document, but the main point is for the cash forecast preparers to gain experience with any permutations in the company's cash flows. The gradual accumulation of knowledge about such matters as the speed with which certain business partners pay the company or cash its checks is key to the improvement of cash forecasts.

> **Tip:** The best time to conduct a cash forecast reconciliation is immediately prior to generating the next forecast, so that any identified issues can be immediately incorporated into the next forecast.

## Summary

A reliable cash forecast is an essential element of every company's operations, since it is needed to anticipate and take action against expected cash shortages. At a minimum, there should be a properly maintained and updated short-term cash forecast that is sufficiently accurate to warn of the timing and amount of a cash shortfall. A medium-term forecast can be added if management needs additional visibility into later periods, though it must understand that the sources of information for a medium-term forecast make it inherently less accurate.

It can take several months to achieve a forecasting process that generates reliable cash forecasts. It is not sufficient to reach this level of success and then move on to other projects. Instead, build review systems that constantly monitor forecasts to see if accuracy levels start to decline, and use this information to correct the forecasting model at once. This high level of watchfulness is needed in every company, since the alteration of company systems that is triggered by new lines of business, new software, acquisitions, and so forth will eventually alter the inputs to the cash forecast, making its results less reliable.

# Chapter 4
## Microsoft Excel Modeling

## Introduction

The Microsoft Excel electronic spreadsheet contains a number of tools that are useful for financial forecasting and modeling. They include the automated calculation of moving averages and exponential smoothing, the creation of trend lines that are based on historical data, and several types of what-if analysis. Some of these tools are available as standard features of Excel, while a few require that the Analysis Toolpak be downloaded. In the latter case, we provide instructions for how to complete the download.

In the following sections, we describe the uses to which these Excel functions can be put, and provide instructions on how to use them.

## Moving Averages Function

A moving average calculation generates a forecast based on the most recent historical information. Excel provides a tool that automatically creates a moving average from this data. To use the moving averages function, it is first necessary to download the function into Excel. To do so, select the **File** tab, then **Options**, and then **Add-Ins**. Select the **Analysis Toolpak** to download the analysis functionality into Excel. Once the toolpak is loaded, follow these steps:

1. Enter on an Excel spreadsheet a series of data points relating to the information to be forecasted. A sample appears below.

| | A | B | C |
|---|---|---|---|
| 1 | | | |
| 2 | | Period | Unit Sales |
| 3 | | 1 | 17,400 |
| 4 | | 2 | 16,900 |
| 5 | | 3 | 17,900 |
| 6 | | 4 | 17,400 |
| 7 | | 5 | 18,300 |
| 8 | | 6 | 16,400 |
| 9 | | 7 | 18,500 |
| 10 | | 8 | 17,700 |

2. Select the **Data** tab and pick the **Data Analysis** option. When the following **Data Analysis** box appears, select the **Moving Average** option and click on **OK**.

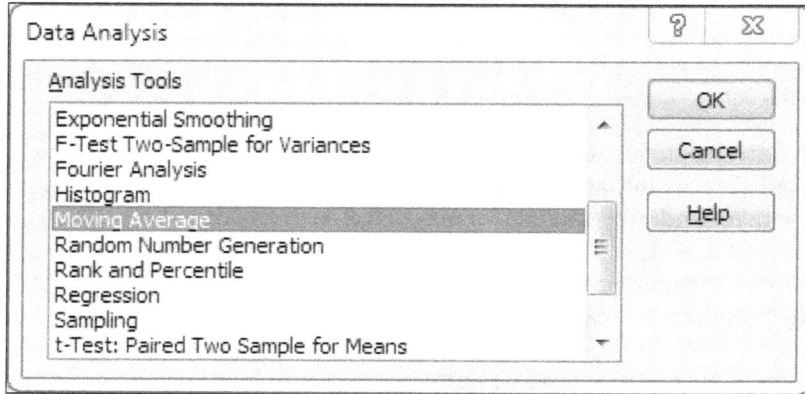

3. The following **Moving Average** box appears. Enter the cell input range (in this case, cells C2 through C10) in the **Input Range**. Enter the cell address range for the resulting moving average (in this case, cells D3 through D10) in the **Output Range**. The completed Moving Average box follows.

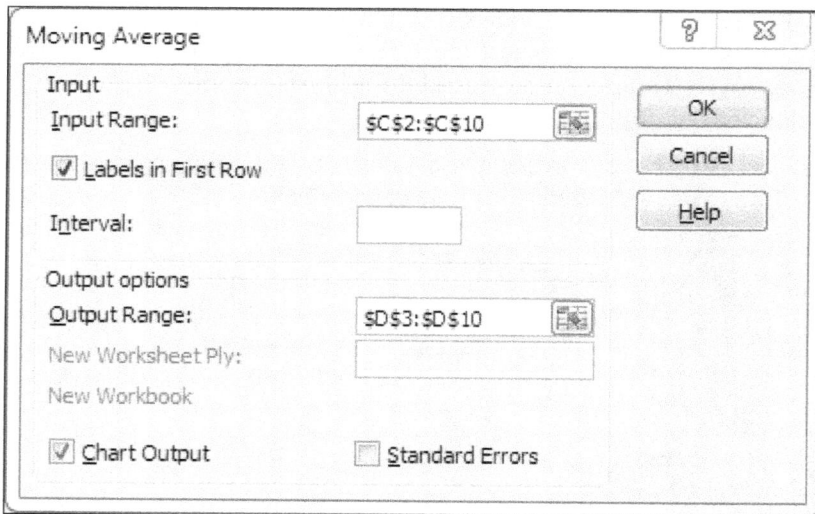

4. Excel automatically creates a moving average based on the listed data, which appears in column D in the following page view, along with a moving average chart. The chart was triggered because we checked the **Chart Output** option in the preceding **Moving Average** box.

| | A | B | C | D | E | F | G | H | I | J |
|---|---|---|---|---|---|---|---|---|---|---|
| 1 | | | | | | | | | | |
| 2 | | Period | Unit Sales | | | | | | | |
| 3 | | 1 | 17,400 | #N/A | | | | | | |
| 4 | | 2 | 16,900 | #N/A | | | | | | |
| 5 | | 3 | 17,900 | 17,400 | | | | | | |
| 6 | | 4 | 17,400 | 17,400 | | | | | | |
| 7 | | 5 | 18,300 | 17,867 | | | | | | |
| 8 | | 6 | 16,400 | 17,367 | | | | | | |
| 9 | | 7 | 18,500 | 17,733 | | | | | | |
| 10 | | 8 | 17,700 | 17,533 | | | | | | |
| 11 | | | | | | | | | | |
| 12 | | | | | | | | | | |

Chart: Moving Average — Value vs Data Point, showing Actual and Forecast series.

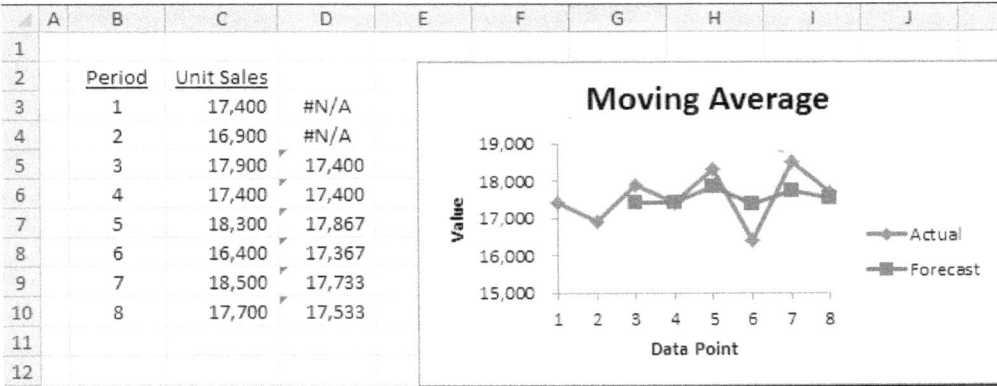

## Exponential Smoothing Function

Exponential smoothing is a variation on the preceding moving average concept, where the key difference is the presence of a *damping factor* in the options that Excel presents. The damping factor is 1 minus the smoothing constant. As we noted in the Financial Forecasting chapter, the smoothing constant determines the level at which actual experience influences a forecast. Thus, if a prior forecast was too high, the smoothing constant is used to reduce the forecast in the next period. Conversely, if a prior forecast was too low, the smoothing constant increases the forecast in the next period. A high damping factor smooths out the peaks and valleys in the data more than a low damping factor.

To use exponential smoothing in Excel, follow the same steps just noted for the moving average function, except you should select the **Exponential Smoothing** option when the **Data Analysis** box appears. Completing the box while using the same data points just noted for the moving average example results in the following entry in the **Exponential Smoothing** box:

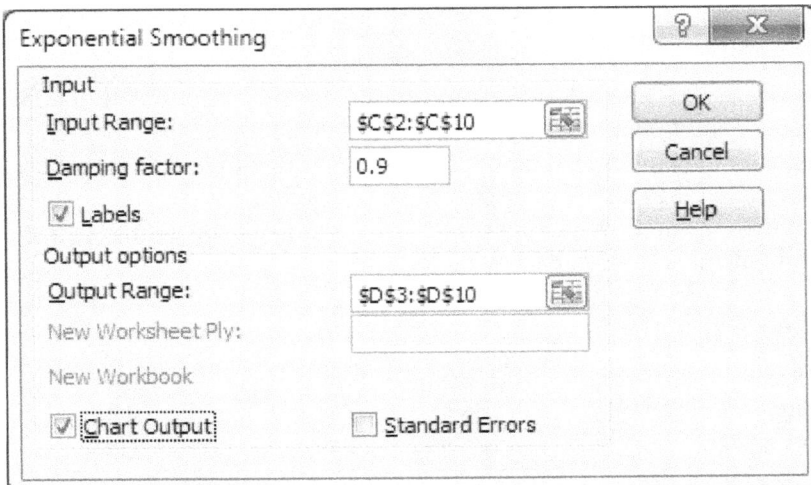

Exponential Smoothing dialog box:

- Input
  - Input Range: $C$2:$C$10
  - Damping factor: 0.9
  - ☑ Labels
- Output options
  - Output Range: $D$3:$D$10
  - New Worksheet Ply:
  - New Workbook
  - ☑ Chart Output
  - ☐ Standard Errors
- OK
- Cancel
- Help

The result of this entry is the following exponential smoothing outcome generated by Excel. Note how the forecast line in the chart is much smoother than was the case with the moving average outcome. This is because the damping factor was set at a high 0.9.

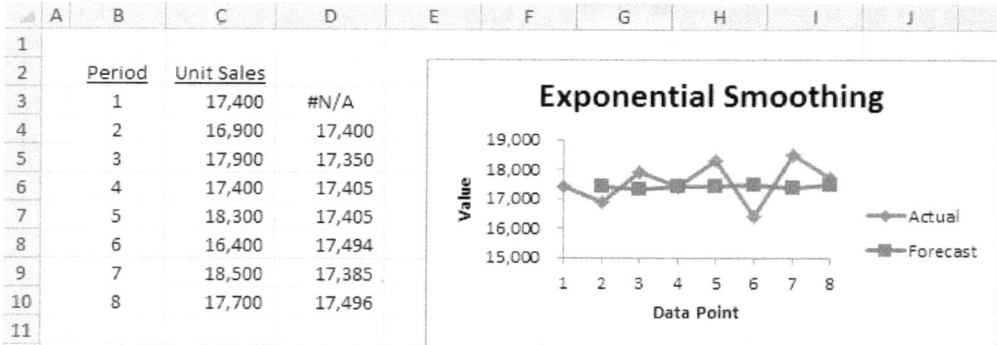

| | A | B | C | D | E | F | G | H | I | J |
|---|---|---|---|---|---|---|---|---|---|---|
| 1 | | | | | | | | | | |
| 2 | | Period | Unit Sales | | | | | | | |
| 3 | | 1 | 17,400 | #N/A | | | | | | |
| 4 | | 2 | 16,900 | 17,400 | | | | | | |
| 5 | | 3 | 17,900 | 17,350 | | | | | | |
| 6 | | 4 | 17,400 | 17,405 | | | | | | |
| 7 | | 5 | 18,300 | 17,405 | | | | | | |
| 8 | | 6 | 16,400 | 17,494 | | | | | | |
| 9 | | 7 | 18,500 | 17,385 | | | | | | |
| 10 | | 8 | 17,700 | 17,496 | | | | | | |
| 11 | | | | | | | | | | |

**Exponential Smoothing** chart (Value vs. Data Point) with Actual and Forecast lines.

If the damping factor had instead been set at a much lower 0.1, the outcome would have been as follows, where the smoothing follows the historical data much more closely.

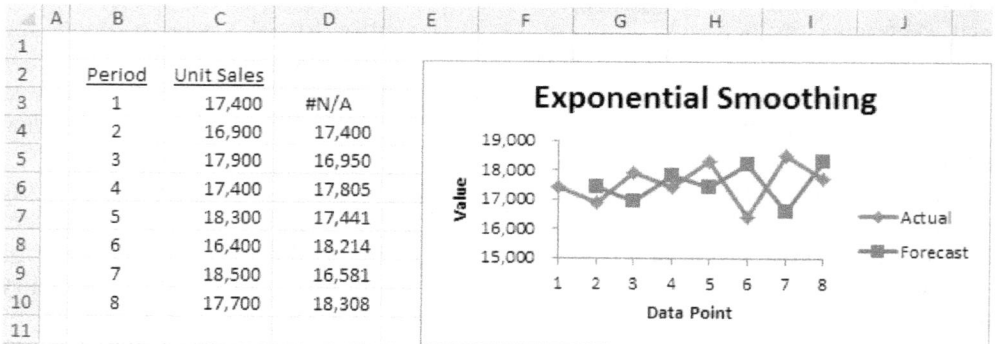

| | A | B | C | D | E | F | G | H | I | J |
|---|---|---|---|---|---|---|---|---|---|---|
| 1 | | | | | | | | | | |
| 2 | | Period | Unit Sales | | | | | | | |
| 3 | | 1 | 17,400 | #N/A | | | | | | |
| 4 | | 2 | 16,900 | 17,400 | | | | | | |
| 5 | | 3 | 17,900 | 16,950 | | | | | | |
| 6 | | 4 | 17,400 | 17,805 | | | | | | |
| 7 | | 5 | 18,300 | 17,441 | | | | | | |
| 8 | | 6 | 16,400 | 18,214 | | | | | | |
| 9 | | 7 | 18,500 | 16,581 | | | | | | |
| 10 | | 8 | 17,700 | 18,308 | | | | | | |
| 11 | | | | | | | | | | |

**Exponential Smoothing** chart (Value vs. Data Point) with Actual and Forecast lines.

## Linear Trend Function

The linear trend function allows one to highlight a set of consecutive numbers and then drag over additional cells. By doing so, Excel automatically calculates the trend associated with the highlighted numbers and extends the trend line into the additional cells. In the following example, the first three (shaded) cells were originally input into a financial model, and then extended with the linear trend function to create the trend appearing in the next three cells.

### Trend Line Calculation

| Historical Period 1 | Historical Period 2 | Historical Period 3 | Projected Period 1 | Projected Period 2 | Projected Period 3 |
|---|---|---|---|---|---|
| 5,000 | 6,200 | 7,000 | 8,067 | 9,067 | 10,067 |

The problem with this dragging function is that the linear trend calculation is not repeated if there is a change in the original data set. Consequently, the drag function is not recommended for high-usage models for which there are expected to be a number of iterations.

An alternative approach is to create a table of all relevant historical values in Excel, plot this information in an Excel chart, and then add a trend line to the chart. The trend line is obtained by right-clicking on the historical data line appearing in the chart and then selecting the "Linear" option. For example, the following time series of data is entered into Excel:

$$3000, 4500, 3800, 5000, 4300, 6100$$

The resulting chart is presented in the following exhibit, along with the associated trend line. Also note that Excel has provided the formula for the resulting trend line within the chart, which is:

$$Y = 460x + 2840$$

The chart also notes that the data has an R value of 0.6642. As noted in the R Value table in the Financial Forecasting chapter, the 0.6642 value indicates a strong positive relationship between the data and the trend line.

**Sample Plot of Historical Data with Linear Trend Overlay**

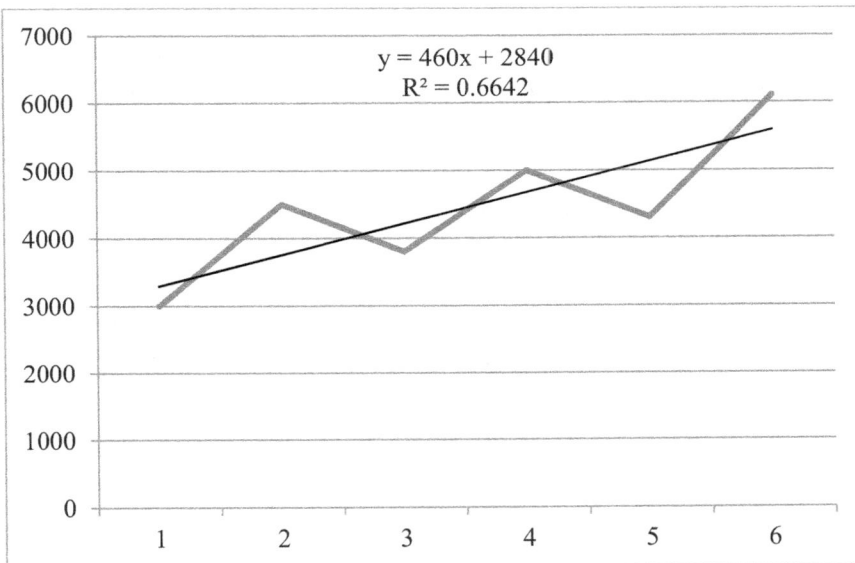

$$y = 460x + 2840$$
$$R^2 = 0.6642$$

## Polynomial Trend Function

A variation on the preceding linear trend function is the polynomial trend, where Excel fits a curved line to the data. This is especially useful when the data presents either an increasing or decreasing pattern. In particular, it can be used to project an accelerating rate of growth or decline in sales.

---

**EXAMPLE**

The Close Call Company's financial analyst is examining the relationship between the organization's investment in fast delivery trucks in a given geographic region and its ability to make deliveries within one hour. The one hour deadline is critical to the company, since it earns an automatic bonus from its customers if it makes the deadline.

An examination of the truck investment finds that a small investment has little impact on the ability of the company to achieve bonuses, since there are too few trucks available to drive to pick up locations and from there to drop off locations. The average transit time is simply too long. At a mid-range level of investment, the company maximizes its bonuses. However, when an area is saturated with trucks, the level of bonus achievement only increases at a minor rate, since only the most distant locations in the region can no longer be reached within the required time limit.

Given this relationship between bonus revenue and truck investment, a polynomial trend line would be the best way to fit a line to the data.

---

As was the case for the Excel linear trend function, relevant historical values can be entered into Excel and then converted into a chart. The trend line is obtained by right-clicking on the historical data line appearing in the chart and then selecting the "Polynomial" option. For example, the following time series of data is entered into Excel:

2500, 3800, 4500, 4750, 4600, 4400

The resulting chart is presented in the following exhibit, along with the associated trend line. Also note that Excel has listed an R value of 0.9863, which indicates a near-perfect fit between the data and the trend line.

**Sample Plot of Historical Data with Polynomial Trend Overlay**

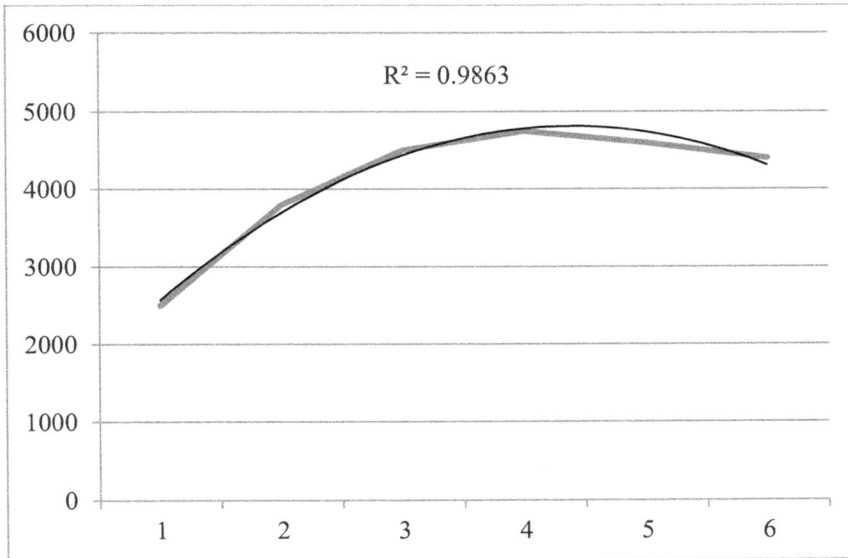

$R^2 = 0.9863$

## Regression Analysis

The preceding linear trend and polynomial trend functions are adequate and efficient tools for calculating a forecast line based on historical data. To gain additional information about the data, the Regression tool is available in Excel.

The regression tool is not immediately available in Excel. To download it, select the **File** tab, then **Options**, and then **Add-Ins**. Select the **Analysis Toolpak** to download the analysis functionality into Excel. Once the toolpak is loaded, follow these steps:

1. Create a data set that itemizes independent and dependent variables for multiple periods. An independent variable is not impacted by any other variables being measured. A dependent variable is impacted by other variables. The following table is an example of such a data set, where we have listed sales (the dependent variable) in the first column, along with the product price and advertising expenditures (independent variables) in the next two columns. We want to see if there is a relationship between the number of units sold and a combination of prices and advertising expenditures.

| ▲ | A | B | C | D | E |
|---|---|---|---|---|---|
| 1 | | | | | |
| 2 | | Period | Units Sold | Price | Advertising |
| 3 | | 1 | 4,250 | $ 4 | $ 5,600 |
| 4 | | 2 | 2,350 | $ 10 | $ 400 |
| 5 | | 3 | 2,800 | $ 6 | $ 800 |
| 6 | | 4 | 3,700 | $ 4 | $ 1,000 |
| 7 | | 5 | 3,100 | $ 10 | $ 6,400 |
| 8 | | 6 | 3,650 | $ 6 | $ 3,600 |
| 9 | | 7 | 2,800 | $ 4 | $ 1,800 |
| 10 | | 8 | 3,250 | $ 5 | $ 2,800 |

2. Select the **Data** tab and pick the **Data Analysis** option. When the following **Data Analysis** box appears, select the **Regression** option and click on **OK**.

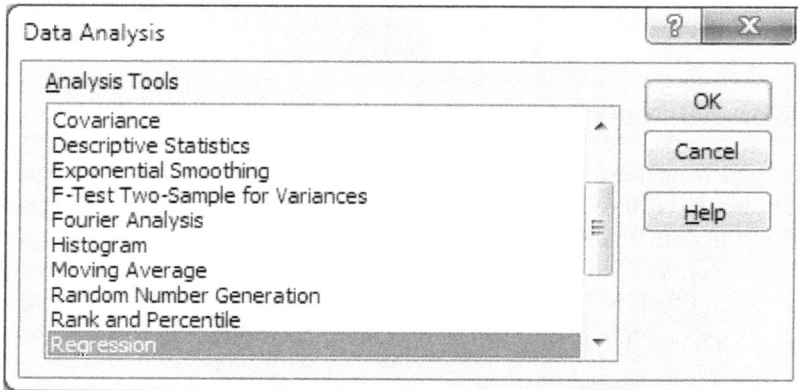

Data Analysis

Analysis Tools

- Covariance
- Descriptive Statistics
- Exponential Smoothing
- F-Test Two-Sample for Variances
- Fourier Analysis
- Histogram
- Moving Average
- Random Number Generation
- Rank and Percentile
- Regression

OK
Cancel
Help

3. The following **Regression** box appears. Enter the cell address range of the dependent variable (in this case, units sold) in the **Input Y Range**. Enter the cell address range of the independent variables (in this case, price and advertising) in the **Input X Range**. Also, select a cell in which the output information will be stated (in this case, just below the data table). The completed **Regression** box follows.

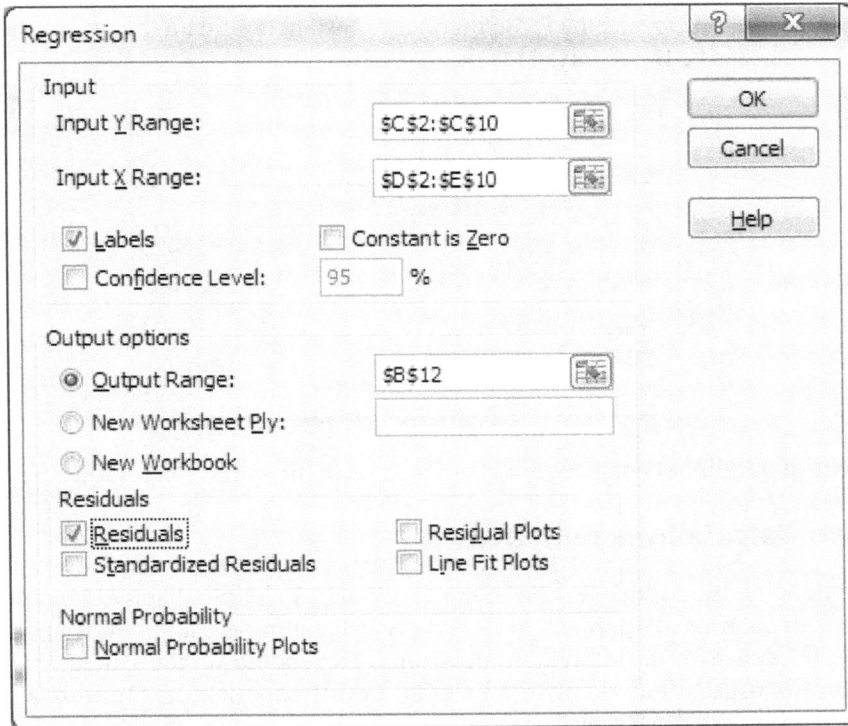

4. Excel automatically creates the following output table. Explanations of the items listed in the table are as follows:

- *Multiple R.* The correlation coefficient (see the Financial Forecasting chapter) between the observed and predicted values. It ranges in value from 0 to 1. A small value indicates that there is little or no linear relationship between the dependent variable and the independent variables. The reported 0.846 indicates the likely presence of a linear relationship.

- *R square.* This is the degree of fit between the line generated from the regression analysis and the source data, which is how well the independent variables explain the dependent variable. The 0.717 value in the table indicates a good fit.

- *Adjusted R square.* This value compares the explanatory power of regression models that contain different numbers of predictors – in this case, there are two predictors, price and advertising. The value gives the percentage of variation explained by only those independent variables that in reality affect the dependent variable. The 0.604 value in the table still indicates a good fit.

- *Standard error.* This value measures the accuracy with which a sample represents a population. This is the standard deviation from the mean of the population.

- *Observations.* This is the number of instances of data that were examined to derive the reported results.

| 12 | SUMMARY OUTPUT | |
|----|----|----|
| 13 | | |
| 14 | *Regression Statistics* | |
| 15 | Multiple R | 0.846916425 |
| 16 | R Square | 0.717267431 |
| 17 | Adjusted R Square | 0.604174403 |
| 18 | Standard Error | 383.3409096 |
| 19 | Observations | 8 |

A number of additional analyses are also reported by this regression tool.

## Iterative Calculations Function

In the Balancing the Model section in the Financial Modeling chapter, we noted that there was an automated approach to iteratively calculating the amount of interest expense associated with the short-term debt plug. Depending on the version of Excel, this option is usually located within the **File** tab. If so, click on **Options** and then **Formulas** to access the **Excel Options** box. Check the box for the **Enable Iterative Calculation** option for the spreadsheet, with the maximum number of iterations set at no more than 100. Once set, Excel will automatically loop through the necessary number of iterations to arrive at the correct balance of interest expense and short-term debt to correctly balance the model. A portion of the **Excel Options** page follows.

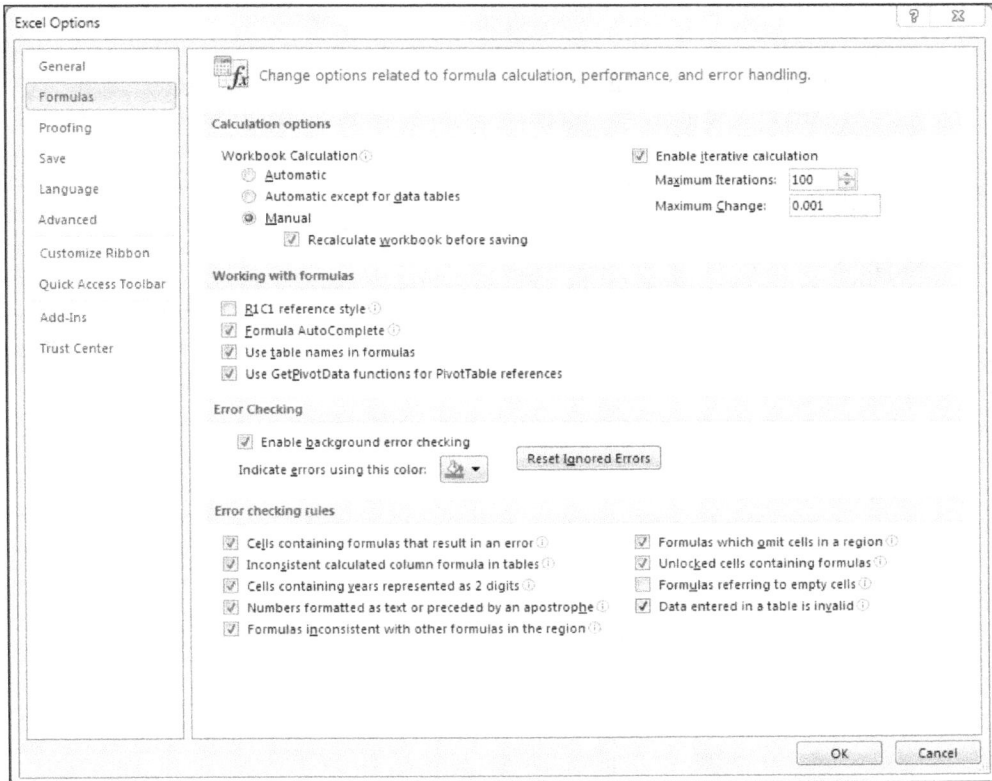

## Data Table

A data table is a range of cells that show how the alteration of one or two variables in a model's formulas will affect the results of those formulas. A data table provides a fast method for the calculation of multiple results, and also provides a consolidated view of the resulting variations. A data table cannot accommodate more than two variables.

A one-variable data table can be used to determine how different values of one variable will alter the results of one or more formulas. Formulas used in this type of table can only refer to one input cell. As an example, a one-variable data table can show how different interest rates alter the amount of a monthly loan payment.

A two-variable data table can be used to determine how different values of two variables in a formula will alter the results of a formula. As an example, a two-variable data table can show how various combinations of interest rates and loan terms alter the amount of a monthly loan payment.

To create a one-variable data table, follow these steps:

1. Enter the list of values to be substituted into the input cell. They can be entered either down a column or across a row. There should be a few empty rows and columns on either side of the values.

2. If the variable values are in a column, type the formula in the cell one row above and one cell to the right of the column of values. If additional formulas are to be used, enter them in cells to the right of the first column.

3. If the variable values are in a row, type the formula in the cell one row to the left of the first value and one cell below the row of values. If additional formulas are to be used, enter them in cells below the first formula. For example, the following extract from a future value analysis shows the inputs to a future value calculation. Cells C4 through C6 display the inputs to the formula, which is located in cell E3. The current solution to the future value of 10 payments of $1,000 at an 8% interest rate is $14,486.56. We want to determine the future value of this stream of payments if the interest rate declines in half-percent increments. The increments appear in column D.

| ◢ A | B | C | D | E |
|---|---|---|---|---|
| 1 | | | | |
| 2 | **Future Value Analysis** | | | FV |
| 3 | | | | $14,486.56 |
| 4 | Rate (annual) | 8.0% | 7.5% | |
| 5 | Number of periods | 10 | 7.0% | |
| 6 | Payment | $   1,000 | 6.5% | |
| 7 | | | 5.0% | |
| 8 | | | 4.5% | |
| 9 | | | 4.0% | |

4. Select the range of cells containing the formulas and values for the analysis.

5. Within the **Data** tab in Excel, click on **What-If Analysis** and then **Data Table** (the exact location may vary, depending on the version of Excel being used).

6. If the data table is oriented as a column, type the cell reference for the input cell in the **Column Input Cell** box. The input box appears in Excel as follows:

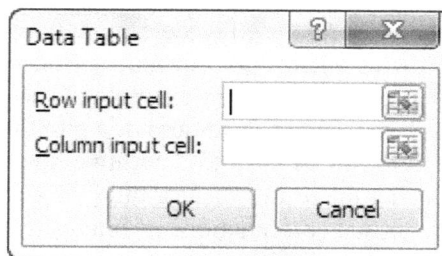

```
Data Table                    ?   X

Row input cell:    |              

Column input cell:                

        OK            Cancel
```

7. If the data table is oriented as a row, type the cell reference for the input cell in the **Row Input Cell** box.

The result of the Data Table calculation appears next, where the full range of possible future values appears in Column E, adjacent to their associated interest rates.

| | A | B | C | D | E |
|---|---|---|---|---|---|
| 1 | | | | | |
| 2 | | **Future Value Analysis** | | | FV |
| 3 | | | | | $14,486.56 |
| 4 | | Rate (annual) | 8.0% | 7.5% | $14,147.09 |
| 5 | | Number of periods | 10 | 7.0% | $13,816.45 |
| 6 | | Payment | $ 1,000 | 6.5% | $13,494.42 |
| 7 | | | | 5.0% | $12,577.89 |
| 8 | | | | 4.5% | $12,288.21 |
| 9 | | | | 4.0% | $12,006.11 |

To create a two-variable data table, follow these steps:

1. Enter the formula that refers to the two input cells into a cell in the worksheet.
2. Enter one list of input values in the same column, situated below the formula.
3. Enter the second list of input values in the same row as the formula, situated to its right. For example, the following extract from a future value analysis shows the inputs to a future value calculation. Cells C4 through C6 display the inputs to the formula, which is located in cell D3. The current solution to the future value of 10 payments of $1,000 at an 8% interest rate is $14,486.56. We want to determine the future value of this stream of payments if the interest rate declines in half-percent increments *and* there are changes in the number of periods. The increments appear in column D. The range of periods over which payments would be made is stated in cells E3 through G3.

| | A | B | C | D | E | F | G |
|---|---|---|---|---|---|---|---|
| 1 | | | | | | | |
| 2 | | Future Value Analysis | | | FV | | |
| 3 | | | | $14,486.56 | 9 | 8 | 7 |
| 4 | | Rate (annual) | 8.0% | 7.5% | | | |
| 5 | | Number of periods | 10 | 7.0% | | | |
| 6 | | Payment | $ 1,000 | 6.5% | | | |
| 7 | | | | 5.0% | | | |
| 8 | | | | 4.5% | | | |
| 9 | | | | 4.0% | | | |

4. Select the range of cells containing the formula, the row and column of values, and the cells in which the calculated values are to be located.
5. Within the **Data** tab in Excel, click on **What-If Analysis**, and then **Data Table**.

6. Type the reference to the input cell for the input values in the row in the **Row Input Cell** box.
7. Type the reference to the input cell for the input values in the column in the **Column Input Cell** box.

The result of the Data Table calculation appears next, where the full range of possible future values appears in Columns E through G, in a matrix format between their associated interest rates and periods.

| | A | B | C | D | E | F | G |
|---|---|---|---|---|---|---|---|
| 1 | | | | | | | |
| 2 | | Future Value Analysis | | | | FV | |
| 3 | | | | $14,486.56 | 9 | 8 | 7 |
| 4 | | Rate (annual) | | 8.0% | 7.5% $ 12,229.85 | $10,446.37 | $8,787.32 |
| 5 | | Number of periods | | 10 | 7.0% $ 11,977.99 | $10,259.80 | $8,654.02 |
| 6 | | Payment | | $ 1,000 | 6.5% $ 11,731.85 | $10,076.86 | $8,522.87 |
| 7 | | | | | 5.0% $ 11,026.56 | $ 9,549.11 | $8,142.01 |
| 8 | | | | | 4.5% $ 10,802.11 | $ 9,380.01 | $8,019.15 |
| 9 | | | | | 4.0% $ 10,582.80 | $ 9,214.23 | $7,898.29 |

The data table concept works best for larger groups of options, since it can take a moderate amount of time to set up.

## Goal Seek

The goal seek function of Excel essentially calculates backwards from a desired financial goal to determine the inputs needed to achieve that goal. By using this tool, one can avoid the tedious high-low method of gradually working toward a solution, instead allowing Excel to solve for the exact solution needed. To conduct a goal seek, follow these steps:

1. Open a new spreadsheet.
2. Enter all of the inputs to an Excel formula. An example appears next, where we have inserted the interest rate, number of periods, and payment that are required for Excel to calculate the future value of a stream of cash payments, using its FV function.

| ⊿ | A | B | C |
|---|---|---|---|
| 1 | | | |
| 2 | | Future Value Analysis | |
| 3 | | | |
| 4 | | Rate (annual) | 8.0% |
| 5 | | Number of periods | 10 |
| 6 | | Payment | $ 1,000 |
| 7 | | Future value | $14,486.56 |

3. Within the **Data** tab in Excel, click on **What-If Analysis**, and then **Goal Seek**.
4. Type the cell address to the **Set Cell** in the **Goal Seek** box. This is the formula to be resolved.
5. Type in the **To Value** field in the **Goal Seek** box the goal for which we are solving. In the following example, we are entering 15000 in the field, since we are trying to arrive at a future value of $15,000.
6. Type in the **By Changing Cell** field in the **Goal Seek** box the reference to the cell that contains the value that we want to adjust. In the example, we want to change the interest rate in cell C4, so that the interest rate is revealed that results in a future value of $15,000. In the example, the Goal Seek function then fills in the two fields with the $15,000 goal and the 8.7% interest rate that is needed to arrive at the $15,000 goal.

| ⊿ | A | B | C | D | E | F | G | H |
|---|---|---|---|---|---|---|---|---|
| 1 | | | | | | | | |
| 2 | | Future Value Analysis | | | | | | |
| 3 | | | | | | | | |
| 4 | | Rate (annual) | 8.7% | Goal Seek Status | | | ? | ✕ |
| 5 | | Number of periods | 10 | | | | | |
| 6 | | Payment | $ 1,000 | Goal Seeking with Cell C7 found a solution. | | | Step | |
| 7 | | | $15,000.00 | | | | Pause | |
| 8 | | | | Target value: 15000 | | | | |
| 9 | | | | Current value: $15,000.00 | | | | |
| 10 | | | | | OK | | Cancel | |
| 11 | | | | | | | | |

## Scenario Manager

The scenario manager tool in Excel can be used to summarize the results of an analysis of the base case, worst case, and best case scenarios (among other alternatives) for an organization. To show how the scenario manager works, we begin with the following analysis of the profitability of a business, where the key variables associated with profitability are the sales level, fixed costs, gross margin percentage, and tax rate. Thus, the model contains four variables.

| ⊿ | A | B | C | D |
|---|---|---|---|---|
| 1 | | | | |
| 2 | | **Scenario Analysis** | | Profits |
| 3 | | | | $ 2,880 |
| 4 | | Sales | $ 210,000 | |
| 5 | | Fixed costs | $ 80,000 | |
| 6 | | Gross margin % | 40% | |
| 7 | | Tax rate % | 28% | |

Using this information as our baseline, we use the Excel Scenario Manager by following these steps:

1. Within the **Data** tab in Excel, click on **What-If Analysis**, and then **Scenario Manager**.
2. The **Scenario Manager** box appears, of which an image appears next.

3. Click the **Add** button to create a scenario, which we will call the Base Case. The following **Edit Scenario** box appears. Enter the cells in which the four variables are located, which are cells C4 through C7. Click on **OK** to complete the entry.

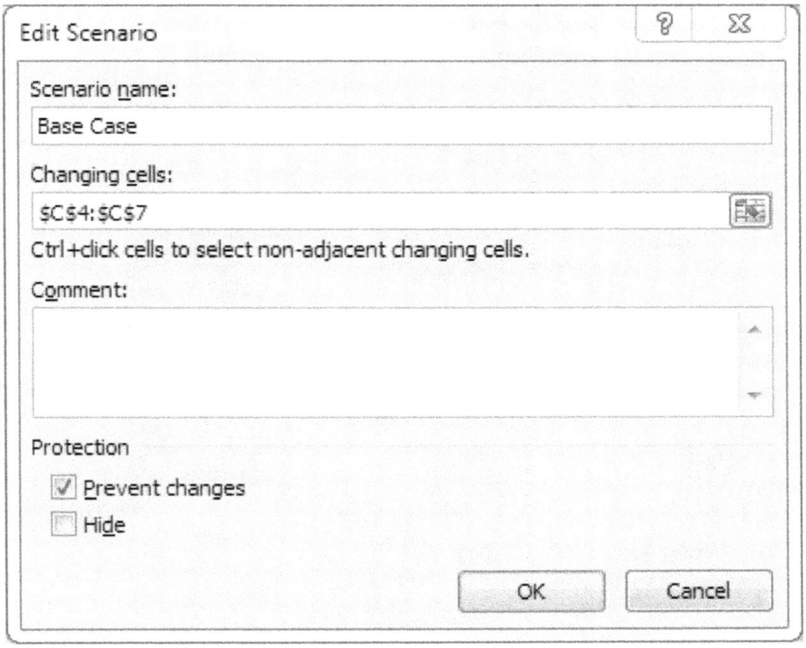

4. The **Scenario Values** box appears. This box autofills with the information initially listed in cells C4 through C7. Press **OK** to complete the base case. The completed box is shown next.

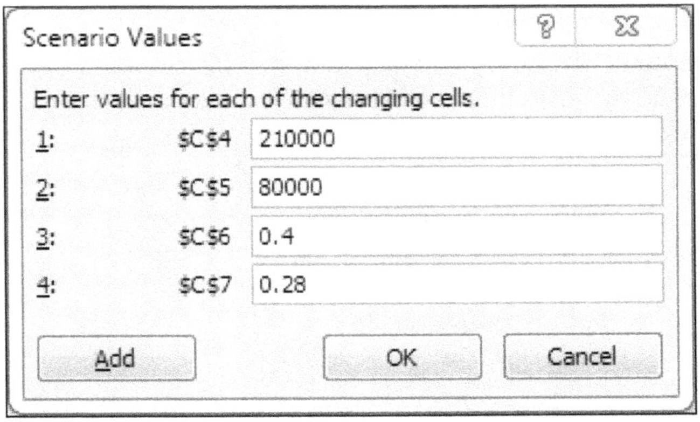

5. Repeat the steps just noted to create a worst case and best case model. We assume that the worst case scenario will experience a sales reduction to $190,000, while management takes action to reduce the fixed cost level down to $70,000. In addition, the gross margin will decline to 38%, and the tax rate will decline to 25% to reflect the reduced earnings of the business. In the best case scenario, sales have increased to $225,000, while fixed costs have increased to $85,000 to support the increased sales. Further, the gross margin has improved to 42%, while the tax rate has increased to 30% to reflect the

increased earnings of the business. The **Scenario Manager** box now contains all three scenarios, as shown in the following graphic.

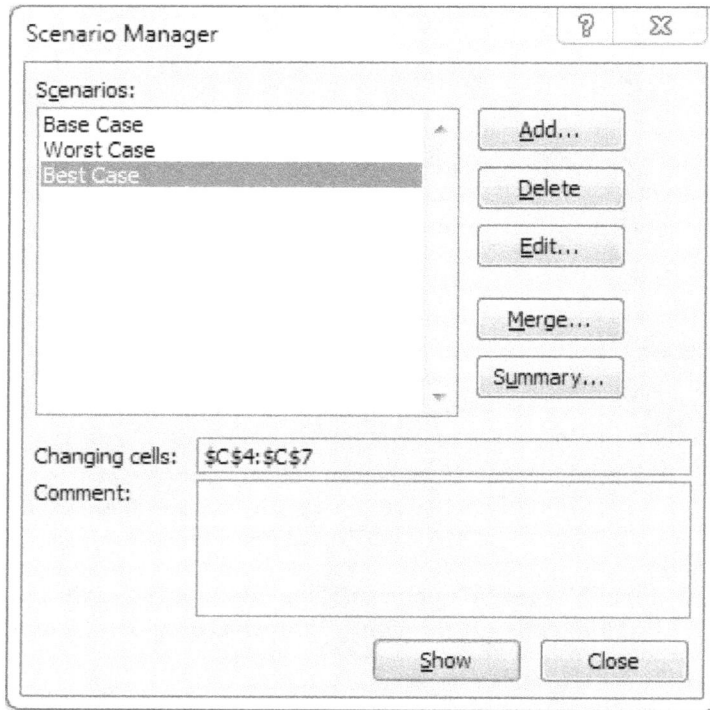

6. The **Scenario Summary** box appears, in which we enter the cell address for the formula that uses the variables to arrive at a profit figure. This entry is cell D3. Click on **OK** to complete the scenario analysis.

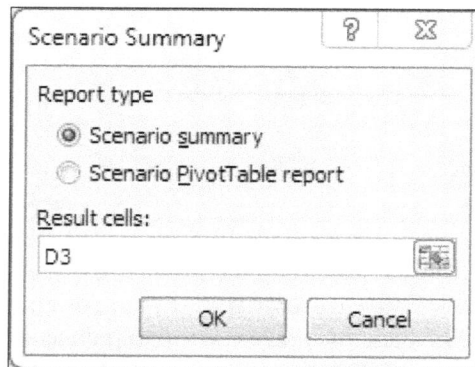

7. Excel creates a summary of all the variables and the related profit outcome on a separate worksheet. The scenario summary shown here is relatively simple. It is possible to use a much larger number of variables within this model.

| | A | B | C | D | E | F | G |
|---|---|---|---|---|---|---|---|
| 1 | | | | | | | |
| 2 | | **Scenario Summary** | | | | | |
| 3 | | | | Current Values: | Base Case | Worst Case | Best Case |
| 5 | | **Changing Cells:** | | | | | |
| 6 | | | $C$4 | $ 210,000 | $ 210,000 | $ 190,000 | $ 225,000 |
| 7 | | | $C$5 | $ 80,000 | $ 80,000 | $ 70,000 | $ 85,000 |
| 8 | | | $C$6 | 40% | 40% | 38% | 42% |
| 9 | | | $C$7 | 28% | 28% | 25% | 30% |
| 10 | | **Result Cells:** | | | | | |
| 11 | | | $D$3 | $ 2,880 | $ 2,880 | $ 1,650 | $ 6,650 |
| 12 | | Notes: Current Values column represents values of changing cells at | | | | | |
| 13 | | time Scenario Summary Report was created. Changing cells for each | | | | | |
| 14 | | scenario are highlighted in gray. | | | | | |

To clean up the model, we can replace the cell references in column C with the names of these cells, as noted in the following improved version of the analysis.

| | A | B | C | D | E | F | G |
|---|---|---|---|---|---|---|---|
| 1 | | | | | | | |
| 2 | | **Scenario Summary** | | | | | |
| 3 | | | | Current Values: | Base Case | Worst Case | Best Case |
| 5 | | **Changing Cells:** | | | | | |
| 6 | | Sales | | $ 210,000 | $ 210,000 | $ 190,000 | $ 225,000 |
| 7 | | Fixed costs | | $ 80,000 | $ 80,000 | $ 70,000 | $ 85,000 |
| 8 | | Gross margin % | | 40% | 40% | 38% | 42% |
| 9 | | Tax rate % | | 28% | 28% | 25% | 30% |
| 10 | | **Result Cells:** | | | | | |
| 11 | | Profit | | $ 2,880 | $ 2,880 | $ 1,650 | $ 6,650 |
| 12 | | Notes: Current Values column represents values of changing cells at | | | | | |
| 13 | | time Scenario Summary Report was created. Changing cells for each | | | | | |
| 14 | | scenario are highlighted in gray. | | | | | |

The number of formulas used in a scenario analysis can be expanded considerably. In the preceding example, we only solved for changes in profitability. However, with additional variables (for which a maximum of 32 are allowed), the analysis could also have included the amount of working capital required, debt required, and earnings before interest and taxes.

The scenario manager is a useful tool for evaluating the risks to which a business is subjected. For more information about risk management, see the author's *Enterprise Risk Management* course.

## Summary

A number of the Excel functions described in this chapter require that data be entered in certain cells in a spreadsheet in a precise manner. This makes the process of setting up an automated forecasting function relatively inefficient and error-prone. Consequently, many of these functions are less useful for short-term "one off" forecasting needs. A better use is to incorporate them into financial models that are expected to be used on a repetitive basis for a long period of time.

The Linear Trend and Polynomial Trend functions are among the easiest of the Excel forecasting tools, being able to produce useful trend lines and formulas within a short period of time. These functions are recommended for short-term analysis purposes.

# Glossary

**A**

*Accounting equation.* The concept that all assets on the balance sheet must equal the total of all liabilities and equity.

**C**

*Capture ratio.* The proportion of customers initially attracted to a company's products that eventually make a purchase.

*Correlation coefficient.* The relationship between an independent and dependent variable.

*Covenant.* A contractual requirement that one party to a contract either specifically complete a task or refrain from doing something.

*Cyclical pattern.* Long-term movements around the trend line that occur over periods of more than one year.

**D**

*Damping factor.* An option in Excel that smooths out the peaks and valleys in the data when using the exponential smoothing function.

*Dependent variable.* A variable that is impacted by other variables being measured.

*Durability bias.* The tendency to project the recent past into the future.

**E**

*Explicit forecast.* A formal attempt to predict future events.

**F**

*Financial model.* A representation of the financial results, financial position, and cash flows of an organization.

*Forecasting.* The prediction of future events.

**I**

*Implicit forecast.* An impromptu forecast that is derived on the spot in order to make a decision.

*Independent variable.* A variable that is not impacted by any other variables being measured.

**L**

*Lagging indicator.* Something that confirms behavior that has already occurred.

*Leading indicator.* Something that can be used to predict future behavior.

## M

*Mid-month convention.* The assumption that assets are always acquired at mid-month for depreciation purposes.

*Moving average.* An average of information derived from the most recent time periods in a data set. The oldest values in the data set are dropped from the average as the data from new time periods are added.

## O

*Order of liquidity.* The presentation of assets in the balance sheet in the order of the time needed to convert them into cash.

## P

*Pacing.* The rate at which operations can be ramped up.

*Pro forma.* Refers to a set of financial statements that incorporate assumptions or hypothetical conditions regarding past or future events.

## R

*R square.* A measure of the degree of fit between the line generated by a regression analysis and the source data.

*Receipts and disbursements method.* A forecast that is based on detailed itemizations of cash inflows and outflows.

*Regression analysis.* A forecasting method that is based on a cause-and-effect relationship between a dependent and independent variable.

## S

*Saturation level.* The point at which all possible buyers have acquired a product.

*Seasonal pattern.* A periodic change that follows a consistent pattern.

*Smoothing constant.* A value that determines the level at which actual experience influences a forecast; used in exponential smoothing.

*Standard error.* A measure of the accuracy with which a sample represents a population.

## T

*Target balance.* A safety stock of cash that is kept on hand to guard against unexpected cash requirements.

*Trend pattern.* A long-term projection of increases or decreases in activity levels contained within the historical information.

*Turning point error.* The failure to predict when a trend will reverse.

## W

*Working capital.* Current assets minus current liabilities.

# Index

Accounting equation............................. 33
Automated cash forecasting................. 76

Balance sheet
    Model ....................................... 49
    Overview of.................................. 33
Budgeting and planning software ......... 65

Capture ratios ...................................... 12
Cash flow information, reliability of .... 77
Cash forecast
    Long-term.................................... 74
    Medium-term................................ 73
    Reconciliation.............................. 79
    Short-term.................................... 69
    Use of averages in ...................... 75
    Variability of ............................... 68
Cash forecasting, automated................. 76
Causal methods...................................... 3
Correlation coefficient.......................... 10
Covenant monitoring............................ 55
Cresting sales........................................ 27
Cyclical component............................... 23

Data table.............................................. 91
Debt modeling ...................................... 53
Delphi method ....................................... 6
Depreciation modeling ......................... 51
Durability bias ...................................... 24

Equity modeling ................................... 54
Explicit forecast.................................... 3
Exponential smoothing.......................... 8
Exponential smoothing function........... 83

Financial modeling
    Inputs.......................................... 45
    Nature of...................................... 42
    Process......................................... 43
Financial statement interactions .......... 41
Fixed asset modeling ............................ 51
Forecast
    Accuracy...................................... 22
    Boundaries................................... 26
    Characteristics ............................. 2

Evaluation ......................................29
Responsibility ................................31
Selection criteria ............................6
Traps ..............................................25
Uses of ...........................................2

Goal seek.........................................94

Implicit forecast .............................3
Income statement
    Format............................................36
    Model.............................................47
Incremental analysis.......................61
Iterative calculations .....................90

Leading indicators..........................21
Linear trend function......................84

Market research...............................5
Model balancing..............................54
Model risk.......................................63
Modeling responsibility .................66
Moving averages.............................7
Moving averages function...............81

Order of liquidity ..........................36
Other assets modeling ...................53

Planning deviations........................25
Polynomial trend function..............86
Pro forma financial statements.......66

Reconciliation of cash forecast .......79
Regression analysis.......................10, 87
Rolling forecast..............................20

Scenario analysis............................60
Scenario manager............................95
Seasonal component........................23
Sensitivity analysis.........................59
Simple forecasting methods ...........13
Smoothing constant........................8
Spending per customer....................18
Statement of cash flows
    Format............................................38
    Model.............................................50

Time series methods ............................... 3
Trend component ................................... 23

Variables in model ............................... 46

Working capital
    Projections ........................................ 56
    Roll forward ..................................... 56